A Message from

Some would question, why this is a 100-day devotional? The parable of the lost sheep sums this up. Is it possible for a Shepherd to leave the majority of his flock behind in search of one lost sheep? The Good Shepherd explains what true love is in this Bible context. Sit tight and get ready to know who He is.

Luke 15:3-7 NLT says, "So Jesus told them this story: 'If a man has a hundred sheep and one of them gets lost, what will he do? Won't he leave the ninety-nine others in the wilderness and go to search for the one that is lost until he finds it? And when he has found it, he will joyfully carry it home on his shoulders. When he arrives, he will call together his friends and neighbours, saying, 'Rejoice with me because I have found my lost sheep.' In the same way, there is more joy in heaven over one lost sinner who repents and returns to God than over ninety-nine others who are righteous and haven't strayed away!

For there is more joy in heaven over one lost sinner returning to God. My prayer is that every life would be blessed as they read this devotional on a daily basis. Draw near to God for a

Spiritual renewal of your thoughts and attitudes. For when Christ meets with you, transformation happens instantly.

Are you where God needs you to be? I pray that He opens your eyes to see the true state of your heart today. David said in Psalm 139:23-24, "Search me, O God, and know my heart; test me and know my anxious thoughts. Point out anything in me that offends you and lead me along the path of everlasting life."

Now is the time to draw near to the Father to truly know Him.

Finally, "I pray for you constantly, asking God, the glorious Father of our Lord Jesus Christ, to give you Spiritual wisdom and insight so that you might grow in your knowledge of God – Ephesians 1:17 NLT".

Be blessed as you meditate on His Word day and night.

Enjoy reading this book

Maria Akande
2021

Table of Contents

A Message from Maria i

Devotional One 1
    Grace to Function 1

Devotional Two 3
    Enter His gates with Thanksgiving 3

Devotional Three 5
    Lead by Example 5

Devotional Four 7
    Are You Ready to Pay the Price? 7

Devotional Five 9
    Let Us Begin to Create 9

Devotional Six 11
    Is Your Position Dormant? 11

Devotional Seven 13
    Be Your Brother's Keeper 13

Devotional Eight 15
    Just Believe! 15

Devotional Nine 17
   Reach Out for Help! 17

Devotional Ten 19
   Where Are You Today? 19

Devotional Eleven 21
   Total Separation 21

Devotional Twelve 23
   Knowing Jesus! 23

Devotional Thirteen 25
   The Unchangeable God 25

Devotional Fourteen 27
   Obedience to the Letter "Go Ye" 27

Devotional Fifteen 29
   The Decisions You Make 29

Devotional Sixteen 31
   Gather All Before the Lord 31

Devotional Seventeen 33
   The Act of Trust 33

Day Eighteen 35
   You Have the Victory! 35

Devotional Nineteen 37
    Give Thanks unto The Lord 37

Devotional Twenty 39
    Persistency in Prayer 39

Devotional Twenty-One 41
    Mercy Availeth Much 41

Devotional Twenty-Two 43
    It Is So 43

Devotional Twenty-Three 45
    Change of Environment 45

Devotional Twenty-Four 47
    Fear Not! 47

Devotional Twenty-Five 49
    What is the Colour of Your Day? 49

Devotional Twenty-Six 51
    The Mystery of Life 51

Devotional Twenty-Seven 53
    Capture the Moment 53

Devotional Twenty-Eight 55
    Set Boundaries 55

Devotional Twenty-Nine **57**
    Your Response 57

Devotional Thirty **59**
    Make A Clean Slate with God 59

Devotional Thirty-One **61**
    Who Is Your Go-To Person? 61

Devotional Thirty-Two **63**
    You Are Called to Serve 63

Devotional Thirty-Three **65**
    Retention 65

Devotional Thirty-Four **67**
    Wrongful Assumptions 67

Devotional Thirty-Five **69**
    Look Forward 69

Devotional Thirty-Six **71**
    A Bright New Day 71

Devotional Thirty-Seven **73**
    Crazy Faith 73

Devotional Thirty-Eight **75**
    Abundance 75

Devotional Thirty-Nine 77
   Don't Get Tired 77

Devotional Forty 79
   Get Back into Action! 79

Devotional Forty-One 81
   Stand Up and Do the Needful 81

Devotional Forty-Two 83
   Despair! 83

Devotional Forty-Three 85
   Ask for Help 85

Devotional Forty-Four 87
   Understanding 87

Devotional Forty-Five 89
   Seasons 89

Devotional Forty-Six 91
   Endurance 91

Devotional Forty-Seven 93
   Stop Shouting 93

Devotional Forty-Eight 95
   God Is So Good 95

Devotional Forty-Nine 97
    Carefully Study Your Actions! 97

Devotional Fifty 99
    Your Position 99

Devotional Fifty-One 101
    Faith 101

Devotional Fifty-Two 103
    Knowledge is Power 103

Devotional Fifty-Three 105
    Decisions Made 105

Devotional Fifty-Four 107
    He Is More Than Able 107

Devotional Fifty-Five 109
    Engagement 109

Devotional Fifty-Six 111
    The Noise is deafening 111

Devotional Fifty-Seven 112
    How Big is Your Dream? 112

Devotional Fifty-Eight 114
    What Do You Have? 114

Devotional Fifty-Nine **116**
    Time Is Ticking! 116

Devotional Sixty **118**
    Who or What Inspires You? 118

Devotional Sixty-One **120**
    Abide! 120

Devotional Sixty-Two **122**
    Revelation! 122

Devotional Sixty-Three **124**
    Knowledge! 124

Devotional Sixty-Four **126**
    What Do You Have in Your Hands? 126

Devotional Sixty-Five **128**
    What Do You Allow into Your Heart? 128

Devotional Sixty-Six **130**
    Are You Firmly Rooted in His Word? 130

Devotional Sixty-Seven **132**
    Amend Bridges 132

Devotional Sixty-Eight **134**
    And this Too Shall Come to Pass 134

Devotional Sixty-Nine 136
    God Is Doing Something New 136

Devotional Seventy 138
    Go Back to the Basics 138

Devotional Seventy-One 140
    Be Inspired 140

Devotional Seventy-Two 142
    Do the Needful and Rest 142

Devotional Seventy-Three 144
    Make an Effort 144

Devotional Seventy-Four 146
    Your Gifts 146

Devotional Seventy-Five 148
    Clear Out the Weed 148

Devotional Seventy-Six 150
    Rainbow 150

Devotional Seventy-Seven 152
    Fight for Your Life 152

Devotional Seventy-Eight 154
    Revert Back 154

Devotional Seventy-Nine **156**
    What Did God Say? 156

Devotional Eighty **158**
    Take Action 158

Devotional Eighty-One **160**
    What Do You Do When the Going Gets Tough? 160

Devotional Eighty-Two **162**
    Sit Down and Get on With It 162

Devotional Eighty-Three **164**
    Is Your Oil Running Out? 164

Devotional Eighty-Four **166**
    Go Tell It on the Mountain 166

Devotional Eighty-Five **168**
    Take Baby Steps 168

Devotional Eighty-Six **170**
    Cleanliness 170

Devotional Eighty-Seven **172**
    Strap Up and Get Ready for the Ride 172

Devotional Eighty-Eight **174**
    Decisions 174

Devotional Eighty-Nine **176**
    Follow Him.. 176

Devotional Ninety.. **178**
    He Said So!... 178

Devotional Ninety-One **180**
    Decisions (2) 180

Devotional Ninety-Two **182**
    Trust the Process.. 182

Devotional Ninety-Three **184**
    How You Enter Your Day Matters............................ 184

Devotional Ninety-Four **186**
    Pick Up Your Phone 186

Devotional Ninety-Five... **188**
    The State of Your Heart... 188

Devotional Ninety-Six **190**
    Take No Offense 190

Devotional Ninety-Seven **192**
    Breathe 192

Devotional Ninety-Eight... **194**
    Change Your Circle... 194

Devotional Ninety-Nine **196**
  Change Your View and Do the Needful 196
Devotional One Hundred **198**
  Go Get It 198
Final Word **200**
Acknowledgement **202**

Devotional One

Grace to Function

¹⁶I pray that from his glorious, unlimited resources he will empower you with inner strength through his Spirit. ¹⁷ Then Christ will make his home in your hearts as you trust in him. Your roots will grow down into God's love and keep you strong. ¹⁸And may you have the power to understand, as all God's people should, how wide, how long, how high, and how deep his love is.

(Ephesians 3:16-18 NLT)

Greetings to you my dearly beloved family in Christ Jesus. For God has given you and I the grace to function aright, therefore rise up and praise His holy name.

For it pleased the Lord to give you and I grace unlimited. Therefore rejoice for greater things are ahead of you. What has the Lord promised to give you? Wait on Him with joy in your heart, for He will do what no man can do. Rise up today!

Psalms 115:17-18 AMP says, "The dead do not praise the Lord, nor do any who go down into silence; But as for us, we will bless and affectionately and gratefully praise the Lord From this time forth and forever. Praise the Lord! (Hallelujah!)"

Determine in your heart to praise Him regardless. His grace is sufficient for you, therefore boast of His greatness. He is a good Father. He knows your very name therefore trust in Him completely!

Rely not on your wisdom if you truly want to come out victorious. O TASTE AND SEE THAT THE LORD IS GOOD. Do not give up on God instead cling unto the faith you profess. He is able to transform that very situation for your good. Keep trusting Him regardless of what the so-called experts say. What is God saying over that matter? Hold on to His promises and receive grace to wait patiently. For His Word will never return to Him void.

Finally, as you wait upon Him, it is important that you fix your eyes completely on Him and no one else. Declare His promises by opening your mouth and quit focusing on the mountain. Praise God for removing every mountain and obstacle on your path and rest in Him. For there is nothing He cannot do. Trust Him completely and lean not on your own understanding.

"Have I not commanded you? Be strong and courageous! Do not be terrified or dismayed (intimidated), for the Lord your God is with you wherever you go." Joshua 1:9 AMP"

Devotional Two

Enter His gates with Thanksgiving

¹⁶See, I have written your name on the palms of my hands. Always in my mind is a picture of Jerusalem's walls in ruins. ¹⁷Soon your descendants will come back, and all who are trying to destroy you will go away. ¹⁸Look around you and see, for all your children will come back to you. As surely as I live," says the Lord, "they will be like jewels or bridal ornaments for you to display.

(Isaiah 49: 16-18 NLT)

Greetings to you my family in Christ. A new day has come, and you are privileged to witness it. Praise God Most High for He is worthy to be praised. Enter His gates with thanksgiving in your heart and come into His courts with praise. Decide to praise God regardless of how tough life might be. Call His attention by praising His Holy name today. For He knows your name and yearns for your undivided attention.

Let's look at the life of Joseph today. He moved from being his father's favourite to slavery before he tasted the victories declared by the Lord. Joseph suffered terribly but appreciated God regardless. Even in Prison, He stood out and was put in charge of all prison matters. Bible says He succeeded in all He did. Not a few but all. He eventually tasted the goodness of God and was made second in command to the King of Egypt. What a leap? That is what God can do if you choose to remain steadfast in prayer with a thankful heart.

Where are you today? Drop all you are doing now and praise God more than ever before. It is time you dream again. Yes, dream big and hold unto God's promises over your life. What did He promise you? Thank Him for all He would do. For He will do great things for you. Just believe!

Finally, decide to remain in that place of thanksgiving from henceforth. Count all your blessings on a daily basis and name them one by one. Do not give in to the lies of the enemy or allow fear to kill your joy. Remember that God's joy is available unto you. Receive it now and remain strong. Keep declaring what you want to see and do not stop until it is manifested! Be persistent in prayer and remember that the Lord is always with you. Something good is coming your way. Just believe!

Devotional Three

Lead by Example

¹⁵So be careful how you live. Don't live like fools, but like those who are wise. ¹⁶Make the most of every opportunity in these evil days. ¹⁷Don't act thoughtlessly, but understand what the Lord wants you to do.

(Ephesians 5:15-17 NLT)

Greetings to you my blessed family in Christ. What legacy will leave behind? What have you deposited thus far?

Many fail to realise their actions are being monitored by God and man. Yes, God knows and sees all but trust me when I say, someone somewhere is watching you. Therefore, how you conduct yourself matters a lot, for you are building someone's idea of life by the way you live yours.

Quit allowing the flesh to drive your actions. You have a choice on a day-to-day basis to either choose right or wrong. Which are you choosing today?

So, you roam around like one untamed believing you are a god in your own right not submitting to anything but your ego and self-righteousness. Wake up now before it's too late! For there are eternal consequences for your actions. Think now!

It's important to know that Christ in you makes you strong and complete. None that you have is down to your ability or might but God's grace and favour. Yes, for it has pleased the Lord to keep you in that state now. Do not grieve the Holy Spirit instead rise up now from your slumber and let God lead you aright.

Finally, for those who are on the path of righteousness, continue to hold firm to the faith you profess. Do not give an opening to the devil, for his plan is to destroy you completely therefore rely not on your own power or might but on the strength and power of the Holy Spirit. For He will show you what way to go. Be persistent in your prayer for the body of Christ. Remember that you have a duty in the Kingdom of Heaven to "Go and make disciples of men".

Rise now and take charge!

Devotional Four

Are You Ready to Pay the Price?

[15]But even before I was born, God chose me and called me by his marvellous grace. Then it pleased him [16]to reveal his Son to me so that I would proclaim the Good News about Jesus to the Gentiles. When this happened, I did not rush out to consult with any human being.

(Galatians 1:15-16 NLT)

Greetings to you my family in Christ Jesus. My prayer is that this message will be shared with those intended by God and that your eyes will be opened to truly see and understand what God is saying.

If you are not ready, I would advise you to stop reading and move on to your regular activities but if you are truly ready, read on.

There is a price to pay for the anointing, there is also a price to pay to truly follow Christ. You cannot come to Him with the baggage you carry and expect to be used by Him. Many are overburdened with traits of self and wonder why they fall continuously. Yes, the righteous fall and rise again but there comes a time when maturity must kick in and this is when you are determined to drop all weights that you might remain standing and manifest all that was intended by God from the beginning of Creation. Discipline and Selflessness are key!

Christ was determined to please the Father and He did. Though He was deeply troubled when He remembered what was at hand, He stuck to the plan and lived a life pleasing to God. Christ submitted to the will of God and not His will. Christ was selfless, He had feelings but submitted not to it. He chose God's plan till the very end and finished the task gracefully. Whose will are you submitting to? Selah

Now is the time to decide what path you choose to follow. Christ Jesus is saying "come, drop your nets and follow me". If you truly want to be His true disciple, there is a price to pay. You must die to self in order to resurrect with Christ as a new creature.

Romans 12: 1 TPT says, "Beloved friends, what should be our proper response to God's marvelous mercies? To surrender yourselves to God to be his sacred, living sacrifices. And live in holiness, experiencing all that delights his heart. For this becomes your genuine expression of worship".

Jesus suffered the pain, torture, mockery, humiliation for you and I to be saved . Decide now and move aright!

Devotional Five

Let Us Begin to Create

¹¹Then God said, "Let the land sprout with vegetation—every sort of seed-bearing plant, and trees that grow seed-bearing fruit. These seeds will then produce the kinds of plants and trees from which they came." And that is what happened.

(Genesis 1: 11 NLT)

Greetings to you my blessed family in Christ Jesus. It is the time and season to create. When all hope is lost and you feel like giving up, trust again! For the time to Create has come.

Let's go on a journey together starting from the creation of the earth. Scripture says in Genesis 1:1 that the earth was without form, void and darkness covered the deep waters. Could this be the state of your mind now? Have you lost the willpower to try or even dream again? Are you at the borderline of ending it all? If this is you, I speak life over you now "LET THERE BE LIGHT".

It is important to note that God existed and was present even in the darkness. What do I mean? For it pleased the Lord to change the condition of the earth by commanding Light into existing. Therefore, cease from your worry and allow this Word of wisdom to resonate in your heart today. For your season of weeping and sorrow is over. Let there be light and there was light! Hallelujah

God is with you even in that low and dark place. He says, " I will never leave you nor forsake you". To shed more light on His unconditional love, He also said that He would leave the ninety-nine behind in search of that one lost sheep. Could this be you? Rise now and dream again.

Many have failed to see the beauty of life due to their experiences thus far. Are you mourning the loss of a loved one or enduring hardship? Please hang in there for help is on the way. The Lord hears your cry and will free you from all your troubles. It is okay to cry but do not tarry there instead choose to see the Light by asking the Holy Spirit for help today.

Light has come and it is time to create again with the help of the Holy Spirit. Remember that the devil kills, steals and destroy all he touches therefore quit entertaining evil thoughts instead choose to think only on what is good, true and right. You have the power to create therefore begin to create with the help of the Holy Spirit. He will comfort you and show you the way to go.

Rise from the dead and come back to life now! God is depending on you!

Devotional Six

Is Your Position Dormant?

¹¹There is much more we would like to say about this, but it is difficult to explain, especially since you are spiritually dull and don't seem to listen. ¹²You have been believers so long now that you ought to be teaching others. Instead, you need someone to teach you again the basic things about God's word. You are like babies who need milk and cannot eat solid food. ¹³For someone who lives on milk is still an infant and doesn't know how to do what is right. ¹⁴Solid food is for those who are mature, who through training have the skill to recognize the difference between right and wrong.

(Hebrews 5:11-14 NLT)

Greetings to you my blessed family in Christ Jesus. Where are you positioned this season? Are you failing to stay in position? Get back in line saith the Lord.

I woke up this morning to find majority of my plates broken. I knew this happened due to my foolishness. I wrongly positioned the plates which led to this accident. Where have you positioned yourself this season? Is it where God has assigned or are you simply doing what seems right, a "hit & miss" approach? It is important you know your divine position in order to live a life pleasing to God Almighty.

Nobody is here on earth by chance. For God has a specific purpose for you on earth and it is only wise to ask the creator for clarity so you can truly please Him. Many would ask for the definition of position in this context. This can be compared to your assignment or seasonal duty. There are times and seasons for everything under the sun therefore what task has the Lord given you to do this season now? Do you have a personal relationship with God or live blindly doing whatever seems right to do?

It is time to intentionally seek God for He is near and mighty to save. Draw close to God that you might receive insight and wisdom to function aright. I was informed that I had left my position unguarded for a while which is disastrous not just for me but for the body of Christ. I am grateful for the reminder today and the nudge to rise again. What about you?

But Christ has rescued us from the curse pronounced by the law. When He was hung on the cross, He took upon himself the curse for our wrongdoing. For it is written in the Scriptures, "Cursed is everyone who is hung on a tree." Galatians 3:13 NLT

Christ being crucified for you and I, was His divine position at that very hour. He had to trade His life in exchange for our lives. At the point of crucifixion, He had the power to avoid the sufferings and the torment, but He didn't. At that very hour, He had to remain positioned to pass the test. Because of this sacrifice, I am free and free indeed!

Act Now!

Devotional Seven

Be Your Brother's Keeper

16And I will ask the Father, and he will give you another Advocate, who will never leave you. 17He is the Holy Spirit, who leads into all truth. The world cannot receive him, because it isn't looking for him and doesn't recognize him. But you know him, because he lives with you now and later will be in you.

(John 14:16-17 NLT)

Greetings to you my blessed family in Christ Jesus. How are you today? Today's message is to encourage you and reassure you that God is still in the business of doing great things. Hang in there!

Many are in need this season and worried. If you are not in this category, you have a big task to do for those in need. Yes, you! It is time you ask the Holy Spirit for guidance on how to help those in need around you. God made provision that you could provide for others. Why then do you store up treasures without lending a helping hand? Give that it might be given unto you. Ask the Holy Spirit to direct you to those in need and show you how to truly be a blessing to them.

Ever made a promise or vow and failed to redeem it due to the current economic situation or forgetfulness? Ask the Holy Spirit to help you remember all promises made so you can fulfil them one by one. Ecclesiastes 5: 2 says "Do not be hasty with your mouth [speaking careless words or vows] or impulsive in thought to bring up a matter before God. For God is in heaven and you are on earth; therefore, let your words be few." Redeem your pledges now! For it is unto God and not man.

As for me and my house, we will serve the Lord. Are you one trusting that a friend or family member would accept Jesus Christ as their Lord and saviour? Be persistent in your prayers and remember that the Holy Spirit is available to help you. Come unto me all ye who are heavily burdened, and I will give you rest saith the Lord of Hosts. Now is the time to engage with the Holy Spirit for help. He will show you the way to go by ordering your steps aright. Engage now!

Join the Holy Spirit movement by sharing this message with friends and family.

Devotional Eight

Just Believe!

²³I tell you the truth, you can say to this mountain, 'May you be lifted up and thrown into the sea,' and it will happen. But you must really believe it will happen and have no doubt in your heart. ²⁴I tell you, you can pray for anything, and if you believe that you've received it, it will be yours.

(Mark 11:23-24 NLT)

Greetings to you my family and friends in Christ Jesus. Today's message is for all who believe that Jesus is mighty to save. Do you believe?

What are you trusting God for this season? Drop it down at His feet and thank Him for answered prayers. I believe that Christ Jesus will tend to your very needs. Do you believe?

What He said He would do is what He will do. Yes, you have waited for a long time, worry no more for help is here to stay. Do you see it? It will be manifested before your very own eyes in Jesus mighty name Amen.

The bible says in Matthew 18:19 "I promise that when any two of you on earth agree about something you are praying for, my Father in heaven will do it for you".

The bible says in this passage that when you pray in agreement with another of the same faith and belief, He will answer your prayers. Who do you call friends? Search your circle thoroughly ensuring that God is the centre of your relationships.

I have chosen to stand on the promises of God today. What about you? Speak forth what you want to see and wait expectantly for the full manifestation. The length of time spent on the queue matters not, for at the appointed time, all you are trusting Him for will be yours.

Trust in the Lord and put your confidence in all that He has promised. You will not suffer anymore. For your season of barrenness and shame has ceased permanently in Jesus mighty name. Are you going through a wilderness experience right now? Raise the matter before the King of Kings and exalt His Holy name. For He has done great things for you. Receive it now and expect the total manifestation of His promises and Word over your life.

Enjoy the rain of increase and multiplication. You are more than a conqueror through Jesus Christ. Rejoice!

Devotional Nine

Reach Out for Help!

¹⁶Make the most of every opportunity in these evil days. ¹⁷Don't act thoughtlessly, but understand what the Lord wants you to do.

(Ephesians 5:16-17 NLT)

Greetings to you my blessed family in Christ Jesus. A new day is here, and you are alive to witness it. Quit looking down on yourself and start believing that You are more than a conqueror through Jesus Christ. Come out!

Come out from falsehood and rise into the truth this day. Quit living a lie instead come clean and ask God for help to continue the race aright. Are you addicted to pornography, masturbation, sexual immorality, lying, deceitfulness etc.? If yes, come and let us pray together. It is time for a Spiritual awakening. The time is now!

Many have bottled up fear and anxiety in their hearts pretending to be on top of things when they really are not. You don't have to pretend anymore my brothers and sisters. Christ Jesus is calling us back to Himself. Let us return to the Lord now that He is near. It is ok to ask for help. Reach out now!

Are you one lost in dark thoughts, consumed by fear and paralysed by the unknown? Rise up intentionally this day. You have the power to rise out of that pit if you choose to. Welcome the Holy Spirit into your heart and ask Him to help you out of the pit and He will. Do not leave Him until He blesses you. Stop allowing the enemy to win over your heart or mind. Fight for freedom now!

Speak or forever hold your peace. As for me, I choose to speak to that mountain, and I say today "Mountain be moved in Jesus mighty name". You have the power to move, crush and paralyse mountains. It is time to practise your in-built gifts and abilities. Quit feeling sorry for yourself instead decide to make this your best year ever. Rise and Overcome! You have the power on the inside of you, use it.

Declare and keep believing until it becomes your reality. Work at it and never give up.

Devotional Ten

Where Are You Today?

¹⁰Whoever abandons the right path will be severely disciplined; whoever hates correction will die.

(Proverbs 15:10 NLT)

Greetings to you my beloved family in the Lord. There is surely a price to pay for the cross therefore arise and march forward into victory.

Many assume the call is for their own benefit but that's a lie. You and I were called to please the Father and there is work to be done for Him. You cannot simply sit down and do nothing.

1 Corinthians 4:11-13, 16 says "To this present hour we are both hungry and thirsty; we are continually poorly dressed, and we are roughly treated and wander homeless. We work [for our living], working hard with our own hands. When we are reviled and verbally abused, we bless. When we are persecuted, we take it patiently and endure. When we are slandered, we try to be conciliatory and answer softly. We have become like the scum of the world, the dregs of all things, even until now. So, I urge you, be imitators of me [just as a child imitates his father]".

When you read this passage, what do you see? One sentence that shouts out to me is "We have become like the scum of the world" and yet Paul encourages you and I to be like him. Jesus was out on the streets moving from village to village spreading the Gospel. He lived days without food because He was at His father's feet teaching the Word. In fact, Scripture says that there was a time when the crowd were with Him for three days without food and he had compassion on them. Is this possible?

There will come a time when our love for the things of this world will decrease and become irrelevant over the things of God. I believe we have entered this season now, but many would fail because of their love for earthly treasures. Jesus instructed us to store up treasures in heaven and not earth. Why then are we fixated on earthly treasures/matters?

I don't believe God is calling you and I to live like scum literally, but He is saying "Now is the time to seek first His Kingdom and all that pertains to it". He says that when we put Him first, He will tend to our business. He will make a way where there is no way and also provide for all our needs if we return to His feet giving Him our undivided attention.

Rise for Jesus!

Devotional Eleven

Total Separation

[1]Unfriendly people care only about themselves; they lash out at common sense. [2]Fools have no interest in understanding; they only want to air their own opinions. [17]The first to speak in court sounds right—until the cross-examination begins.

(Proverbs 18:1-2, 17 NLT)

Greetings to you my blessed family in Christ. Today's message is titled: Total Separation. What is required for absolute separation?

God instructed Abram in Genesis 12:1 "Go away from your country, and from your relatives and from your father's house, To the land which I will show you".

Many would question why. It is important to know who is Lord over your life. When God speaks, you move but I understand when you say you are not sure who spoke to you. Let us sit here and reflect on this scripture.

Now, God told Abram to leave all he knew, his comfort zone and familiar territory to go on a journey with Him. Abram obeyed however he took with him Lot who was later separated from Him. On this journey with God as King and Lord over your life, you must get to a place of total surrender i.e., total yieldness and obedience to God. It is not enough to take steps partially on this journey. When God instructs, ask for help and walk obediently in a timely manner. It is important to also know that He called you on this journey and will make adequate provision for the journey ahead. Therefore, trust in Him completely even if the assignment sounds foolish.

God needs you and I to surrender but remember that it' is impossible to surrender with a load of weights on your shoulder. Drop the load and walk with God today. Drop the doubts and worry, yield completely to His commands. To know Him more requires sacrifice from your end. He will no longer feed you like a baby. Now is the time to GROW. You must decide to work at it in order to eat this season.

Remember that an idle mind is the devil's playground. Therefore, work out your own salvation with fear and trembling. Yield only to the voice of the Master and walk in truth. Spend quality time with God in order to hear Him aright.

Waste no more time!

Devotional Twelve

Knowing Jesus!

¹³Until I get there, focus on reading the Scriptures to the church, encouraging the believers, and teaching them.

(1 Timothy 4:13 NLT)

Greetings to you my beloved family in Christ Jesus. Are you in the waiting room over a particular matter? Trust that the good Lord will meet you at the point of your need. And so, shall it be. Amen.

I have come with good news for all who are ready to receive from God today. With God, all things are possible so why do you fear? If you have God by your side, all things will work together for your good. Why not just watch how your life plays out? As for me, I have come to a place of REST. All I have is God and all I need is God. That is enough for me. What about you?

Alone you came to this world and alone you will depart from this world. You must decide what path you want to take. It is either light or darkness. The minute you accept Jesus as your Lord and Saviour, you have direct access into the throne room of Grace.

What does it truly mean to accept Jesus Christ as your Lord and Saviour? I am afraid to say that accepting Jesus is more than just confessing in public that He is your Lord and Saviour. You need to come to a place of repentance and total submission.

You must determine in your heart to follow Him all the days of your life by surrendering completely to His Word and will.

As for me, I have come to know that without Him I am nothing. He knows and sees all. He is able to save me from every pit of pain and disaster. What more do I need? He is the Way, the Truth and the Life. All who come to know Him enjoy the abundance of rest and eternal life. I am complete with Jesus. For in Him I move and have my being.

The time has come to decide what path you truly want to take. If Jesus is your Lord and Saviour, why then do you confer with so-called experts before you consult Him? Shouldn't Jesus be your only point of contact? Ponder on this today! You claim to love Him but go to other mediums for help when in desperate need. Is your love for Him real? The time has come to check the true state of your heart.

My prayer is that you will truly see the light and be free indeed!

Devotional Thirteen

The Unchangeable God

¹¹Should you talk that way, O family of Israel? Will the Lord's Spirit have patience with such behaviour? If you would do what is right, you would find my words comforting. ¹²"Someday, O Israel, I will gather you; I will gather the remnant who are left. I will bring you together again like sheep in a pen, like a flock in its pasture. Yes, your land will again be filled with noisy crowds!

(Micah 2:7, 12 NLT)

Greetings to you my beloved brothers and sisters in Christ. For God has not given you the Spirit of fear but that of love and a sound mind. You have a sound mind therefore rest in His Word today. God has not brought you this far to disappoint or fail you therefore rejoice for your light has come.

Arise from your sleep and see the beauty of God all around you. What a mighty God I serve. Do you know the God you serve? He brings order to things that are disorganised and chaotic. What is the state of your heart today? Receive insight and clarity this day in the mighty name of Jesus amen.

What is the divine order of things? When you rise, look to the heavens and thank God for who He is and all that He has done for you regardless of the storm or wind that bloweth around you. Count it all joy for the Lord knoweth and understandeth all things. He has made today possible for you to witness and experience. Give Him all the glory.

Look to the heavens, thank God for His love and blessings over your life. Put on the full armour of God (Read Ephesians 6: 10-17) then pray persistently for all your brothers and sisters in the world. For many are facing trials and tribulations this very hour. Pray in the Spirit always and ensure you follow the direction of the Holy Spirit. For He will lead and show you the way to go.

Now that you have these nuggets, be sure that you will truly reap good fruits If applied well. Complain no more instead remain thankful for God watcheth over you. For things are working together for those who trust in the Lord. Put your faith in Jesus and He will grant you peace and wisdom to function.

Be positioned aright this day with your eyes fixed on Jesus Christ. He is mighty to save you. Hallelujah!!!!

Devotional Fourteen

Obedience to the Letter "Go Ye"

¹¹Because we understand our fearful responsibility to the Lord, we work hard to persuade others. God knows we are sincere, and I hope you know this, too. ¹⁷This means that anyone who belongs to Christ has become a new person. The old life is gone; a new life has begun!

(2 Corinthians 5:11, 17 NLT)

Greetings to you my blessed family in Christ Jesus. Today is here again and you are privileged to witness it. Make it count regardless of the test and trial you are facing. Count your blessings and name them one by one.

The instruction to every believer is "Go ye therefore into the world and make disciples of men". What does this mean? How do you move if you have nothing to give? The truth of the matter is that the minute you accept Jesus as Lord and Saviour, the Holy Spirit becomes part and parcel of you. For He dwells with you continually ready and available to teach you for the task ahead. It is important to note that the bible is the manual for every child of God however it can't be read like a mere book but read through the help and guidance of the Holy Spirit who will navigate you to the secrets in the Word.

Come forth and lean towards the Holy Spirit for help today. He will counsel and show you the way to go. Jesus sent His disciples in pairs, anointing and giving them specifics for the task ahead. My brothers and sisters, you cannot pass this assignment without the help of the Holy Spirit. He will show how to live right on a day-to-day basis pleasing the Father.

Many use the phrase "now is the time". Do you understand what it means in this context? It means today is another opportunity to act right through your engagement with the Holyspirit. Humble yourself today and ask for help. Pray to the Father and He will hear your cry. Ask for help to go about doing His will on a day-to-day basis. Never assume you know the way to go instead cling unto God and move as He leads. He will guide you through. Speak and move as He instructs, and you will finish well. Yield that He may be pleased.

God bless and keep you all. Share and bless lives.

Devotional Fifteen

The Decisions You Make

¹⁷He put on righteousness as his body armour and placed the helmet of salvation on his head. He clothed himself with a robe of vengeance and wrapped himself in a cloak of divine passion. ¹⁸He will repay his enemies for their evil deeds. His fury will fall on his foes. He will pay them back even to the ends of the earth.

(Isaiah 59:17-18 NLT)

Greetings to you my blessed family in God. For it is a new day, thank God for His goodness endures forever. For it has pleased the Lord to grant you and I life today. Glory be to God Most High.

What decisions have you made or what are you on the verge of doing? Now is the time to pause in order to get clear direction from God Almighty for the journey ahead. For the steps of the righteous are ordered by God therefore move as directed. If God is truly your Lord and King, submit to His lordship and move as led.

God is calling you and I back to Himself. For you have taken matters into your hands till date. This can no longer continue if you truly desire to see the wonders and greatness of God in your life. Remember that there is a time and place for everything. It is important that you are in a position for the blessings assigned to you this season. Therefore, retract and reattach yourself to the Holy Spirit this season.

O that you might know the Lord and the power of His Glory.

The Holy Spirit is God's Spirit in operation. For the bible says He dwells in you and I continually, from the minute you accept Jesus Christ as your Lord and Saviour. Now that the Holy Spirit is in operation, you no longer move as before. Ask and ye shall receive. Allow Him lead your decisions and He will show you the way to go. Humble yourself and pray!

For death and life are in the power of the tongue therefore begin to speak life into your future. Speak what you want to see. Allow no negative thoughts to flood your mind instead think only about what is good, right and true. Manage and attentively monitor what comes into your subconscious mind for it's the gateway to your soul.

Arise now and obtain favour from God this day. Begin to possess all that is yours. Remember your bloodline is connected to Abraham.

Reach out and grab all that is yours today.

Devotional Sixteen

Gather All Before the Lord

¹⁷"As for you, if you faithfully follow me as David your father did, obeying all my commands, decrees, and regulations, ¹⁸then I will establish the throne of your dynasty. For I made this covenant with your father, David, when I said, 'One of your descendants will always rule over Israel.'

(2 Chronicles 7:17-18 NLT)

Greetings to you my beloved family in Christ Jesus. Today is a great day packed full of riches and goodness. Believe it and receive all you need now.

How clean is your robe? Ever seen a new white robe? Imagine wearing it and coming in contact with something dirty, what precautions would you need to take to ensure your robe stays white and unstained? It is the same with your spiritual life. Resist the enemy and He will flee!

Who do you dine with? Who do you call friends? What association do you keep? Carefully examine your surroundings and ask the Holy Spirit for the ability to see aright. All things become clear when you walk with the Holy Spirit. Allow Him to open your eyes to see the true intent of all you hang around so you can separate yourself from those who live in darkness. Ask God for help to break all relationships that are unholy and unjust.

Now that your garment is without spots, approach the throne room of grace and obtain favour from God. Bring all the barrels you have and place them at the feet of Jesus; for He will fill as many are placed before Him. How hungry are you for the things of God? The hungrier you are, the more He will feed you. Come and drink from the well that never runs dry. There is abundance when you walk with Christ Jesus.

Hymn: Tis so sweet to trust in Jesus, just to take Him at His Word, just to trust upon His promise, just to know thus saith the Lord.

As you meditate on the lyrics of this hymn. Count your blessings and name them one by one. For it has pleased the Lord to bless you beyond your expectations. Embrace the blessings He has for you this day and expect the manifestation of His promise. It will surely come to pass if you believe and hold on to His Word.

Step unto the path of righteousness and eat of the fruits thereof.

Devotional Seventeen

The Act of Trust

⁶Only a few of its people will be left, like stray olives left on a tree after the harvest. Only two or three remain in the highest branches, four or five scattered here and there on the limbs," declares the Lord, the God of Israel. ⁷Then at last the people will look to their Creator and turn their eyes to the Holy One of Israel. ⁸They will no longer look to their idols for help or worship what their own hands have made. They will never again bow down to their Asherah poles or worship at the pagan shrines they have built.

(Isaiah 17:6-8 NLT)

Greetings to you my beloved family in Christ Jesus. Again, you are blessed with the gift of life. Rise and give thanks to Almighty God for His love and protection over your life.

Have you ever started a task with so much zeal and fire but end up tired and unable to complete it as planned? The Holy Spirit reminded me today that it is not by my power or might that I do that which I have set out to do. For I must remember that He is in charge and allow Him lead and drive the ship to its final destination.

So here I am today encouraging you. Is this the situation you find yourself in today? Have you been on that lane for long and now too tired to complete it? Ask the Holy Spirit for help now. He is readily available to take control and ease the load. Drop it all at His feet and He will carry you from that path of weakness to a place of completion and satisfaction. Trust in Him!

Are you not tired of taking matters into your hands? As for me, I have handed it all to the Holy Spirit. A cry is heard today, and it is for the weary and lost, those who unknowingly took over the control of their lives from the hands of the Holy Spirit and have now fallen along the roadside. Allow the Holy Spirit to steer you into position again. Trust His leadership and He will lead you to the expected end. By so doing, the weight on your shoulders would be lifted suddenly enabling you to fly like an eagle.

The weight holds you back. Drop it all down now and let the Holy Spirit take over. For on this journey of salvation, you must travel light in order to get to the finish line. You will end well in Jesus mighty name amen.

Have a blessed and fulfilled day.

Day Eighteen

You Have the Victory!

¹¹This was his eternal plan, which he carried out through Christ Jesus our Lord. ¹²Because of Christ and our faith in him, we can now come boldly and confidently into God's presence. ¹³So please don't lose heart because of my trials here. I am suffering for you, so you should feel honoured.

(Ephesians 3:11-13 NLT)

Greetings to you family in Christ Jesus. How are you today? Rise up this day knowing that the grace of God is sufficient for you. You are no longer a slave of fear therefore refuse to go into alliance with the devil by accepting and believing his lies. You are beautifully and wonderfully made, set apart for greatness and this is the truth.

Now to those struggling to take Him at His Word, I pray this day that you begin to see God as the Almighty and Waymaker. For He holds the key to your life. My prayer is that you will truly experience the power of Yahweh this season. And this shall be your reality in Jesus mighty name Amen.

You see, I don't just serve any god. For the God I serve is strong and mighty. He is mighty in battle. The one and true God who knows and sees all. For nothing catches Him by surprise.

When God leads you on a familiar or unfamiliar path, ensure that you follow Him completely. Be ye not tempted to go about things using your own understanding instead rely completely on His leading. Yes, this might be hard for many as it is an unfamiliar territory, but He says, "Trust me with all your heart and lean not on your own understanding". For by so doing, you will truly live a victorious life. He knows best, it pays to trust Him completely.

I shout aloud from the mountaintop this day saying, "Jesus Christ is truly Lord and Saviour of the whole universe". He saved you and I and it is because of His sacrifice that we can boldly approach the throne room of Grace. Therefore, run into the throne room of Grace and obtain mercy and favour from the Lord.

He is Yahweh!

Devotional Nineteen

Give Thanks unto The Lord

¹Let all that I am praise the Lord. O Lord my God, how great you are! You are robed with honour and majesty. ²You are dressed in a robe of light. You stretch out the starry curtain of the heavens; ⁴The winds are your messengers; flames of fire are your servants.

(Psalms 104:1-2, 4 NLT)

Greetings to you my family in Christ Jesus. Give Thanks to the Lord for He is good and His mercies endureth forever. Shout His praises above the hills declaring that Jesus is Lord over your life and all that concerns you. Run away from the pit of discouragement and exhaustion and enter into His rest today.

Who are you and what God do you serve? Ask the Holy Spirit to reveal your true identity to you. Many times, we live fake lives following the customs and ways of this world. We find our identity in the description provided by others. We do things out of compulsion rather than commitment. Silence the noise today and step into God's marvellous light.

God's marvellous light opens you to the knowledge of the truth which sets you free from every bondage and entanglement of sin. For you are a child of God therefore you must function as intended by God. Look at the lives of the Pharisees and Sadducees in the time of Jesus's existence on earth. From the minute they heard about Jesus, they started plotting evil against Him. They couldn't accept His light. They read the scriptures, prayed to God religiously but didn't know the God they served. They had slipped into darkness without knowing it.

They had accepted the lies of the enemy without their knowledge. They were blind and deaf to the truth but did not know it. What is it you are unable to see today? Receive clarity and understanding now in Jesus mighty name.

Enter His gates with thanksgiving in your heart. Thank God for redeeming the time and restoring your life. O that you might see the goodness of the Lord in your life whilst you are living. For the Lord is good and His mercies endureth forever. Seek Him whilst He is near. Run not from your calling instead embrace it and run the race set before you with joy and gladness in your heart. For it has pleased the Lord to call you His own. Hallelujah! You did not choose Him, He chose you. Therefore, serve Him wholeheartedly from this day henceforth.

Devotional Twenty

Persistency in Prayer

17This means that anyone who belongs to Christ has become a new person. The old life is gone; a new life has begun! 18And all of this is a gift from God, who brought us back to himself through Christ. And God has given us this task of reconciling people to him. 19For God was in Christ, reconciling the world to himself, no longer counting people's sins against them. And he gave us this wonderful message of reconciliation. 20So we are Christ's ambassadors; God is making his appeal through us. We speak for Christ when we plead, "Come back to God!"

(2 Corinthians 5:17-20 NLT)

Greetings to you my beloved family in Christ. Again, you are privileged to see a new day. All the glory belongs to God Most High. Hallelujah!

Ever imagined that breakthrough coming to pass? I personally believe many of our prayers fail to manifest before our eyes because of unbelief. So, you present a matter before God Almighty but doubt that it is possible. Why would He grant you that desire, if you already believe it is impossible to be met? It is time to be persistent in prayer in order to truly know the true intent of your heart.

Who is God to you? Many pray to Him but doubt that He exists because of their many failures. In fact, many believe He is blind to their pain and deaf to their cry. This is another lie from the pit of hell. Step out of darkness today and enter His marvellous light.

For God is true to all He says. He never ignores His promises. For all He has promised that He will do. Scripture says "His Word will not return to Him void" therefore if you are facing many trials, ask the Holy Spirit to open your eyes to the main cause or root of the issue. You can access the truth by engaging with the Holy Spirit.

Who is the Holy Spirit to you? He is God's Spirit on the inside of those who live in the truth. Do you believe that Jesus Christ is God's own Son who died for your sins? Do you believe? Your eyes will see, and your ears will hear aright. Thus, saith the Lord.

Remain in His truth and persistent in prayer.

Devotional Twenty-One

Mercy Availeth Much

17Morning, noon, and night I cry out in my distress, and the Lord hears my voice. 18He ransoms me and keeps me safe from the battle waged against me, though many still oppose me. 22Give your burdens to the Lord, and he will take care of you. He will not permit the godly to slip and fall.

(Psalms 55:17-18, 22 NLT)

Greetings to you my family in Christ Jesus. For the mercy of God is available for those who need it. Ask and you shall receive His mercy today. Life is here in abundance, make every attempt to enjoy it. Quit murmuring and complaining instead give thanks unto God.

Rise up from that pitiful state and declare that Jesus Christ is Lord over your life. Are you faced with a test or trial? Rise and place that matter before God, with thanksgiving in your heart knowing and trusting that God has heard your cry. Knock until the door is open unto you.

What is that troubling matter before you? Is it bigger than your God? Many say you cannot understand until you have gone through a similar trial, but I beg to differ. I don't need to go through your pain to understand what you are going through because the one who knows and sees all things is very much alive and present. He knows your name and knows exactly where it hurts. He is mighty to save those who put their trust in Him. Trust and obey!

As for me and my house, we shall continuously abide under God's mercy. His mercy keeps and protects us from harm. What a great place to be. For under His wings, we lay. What about you? Selah

God has a plan and a purpose for your life. Therefore, be ye not discouraged and disheartened, for God did not bring you this far to leave you. Seek His face and He will come to your rescue.

Rise knowing you have a God who is able to turn things around for your good. You will come out victorious in Jesus mighty name Amen. Declare God's mercy over your life and wait expectantly.

Come into the family of love and peace today by accepting Jesus Christ as your personal Lord and Saviour.

Devotional Twenty-Two

It Is So

¹¹So if the old way, which has been replaced, was glorious, how much more glorious is the new, which remains forever! ¹²Since this new way gives us such confidence; we can be very bold. ¹⁷For the Lord is the Spirit, and wherever the Spirit of the Lord is, there is freedom.

(2 Corinthians 3:11-12, 17 NLT)

What is that which God has spoken over your life? We have come to a time and age when many voices speak over or around us. It is important to discern the Spirit behind every voice so that you remain standing at the end of the battle.

For greater is He that is in you than He that is in the world. Therefore, fear not! Rise up from the place of discomfort and unrest today and enter into His marvellous rest i.e., worry not about a thing instead place it all at His feet believing that He has things under control. Trust wholeheartedly for He is at work in your life.

Come ye who have ears, come ye who have eyes and yearn for more of Him. Come today and receive light from His throne room of grace. For there is a fresh unction upon those who truly desire the manifestation and overwhelming power of the Lord. You have prayed for the ability to see deeper things, why not thank Him for the little you can see i.e., the birds of the air, the trees in the field and the beautiful world He has placed you in. Start small by appreciating what you see around you. The more you appreciate the little, the more He blesses you with more, increasing your capacity to see bigger and experience greater things.

To you who are tired and almost at the edge of giving up, don't you dare give any room to the devil. What are the voices that speak to you? Many kill time by watching all sorts of movies, many surf the internet running into demonic territories unknowingly then wonder why things are not working out for them. Remember that the Bible says, "Guard our hearts with all diligence, for out of it are the issues of life". Run far away from unknown territories and noise. Not everything that sounds good is actually good. Ask the Holy Spirit for the grace to discern and truly know the source of every voice or sound projected to/around you. Close your ears to the noise that comes from the camp of the enemy.

Finally, ask for the grace to remain standing through every trial and temptation. Stand boldly knowing that God has your back. Hallelujah

Devotional Twenty-Three

Change of Environment

17Those others do not have pure motives as they preach about Christ. They preach with selfish ambition, not sincerely, intending to make my chains more painful to me. 18But that doesn't matter. Whether their motives are false or genuine, the message about Christ is being preached either way, so I rejoice. And I will continue to rejoice. 19For I know that as you pray for me and the Spirit of Jesus Christ helps me, this will lead to my deliverance.

(Philippians 1:17-19 NLT)

Greetings to you my Brothers and Sisters in Christ Jesus. Allow not your environment to change your confession. Who do you say that God is? Do you proudly declare the name of Jesus or hide in fear due to the condition or state of the environment you find yourself in? For the time has come to boldly represent the one you claim to serve.

It is important that you begin to see yourself as a vessel created to serve the Most High God. You must represent light wherever you are placed if you are genuinely His child. It is no longer good enough to simply call on Him whenever it suits you because of your pressing needs. You must develop a 1-1 relationship with God if you truly want to know Him.

For the Lord longs for your undivided attention. He calls upon those who are ready for change. Come now and receive life saith the Lord of Hosts. Are you feeling frustrated and unable to function? Take it to the Lord in prayer. What is that mountain that stops you from abiding and truly living as you ought to? Ask God for help today and He will move that mountain in your favour.

Draw near to God that He may draw near to you. Are you able to look away from that mountain and focus on God regardless? Are you thirsty for more of Him and in need of a divine encounter with the King of Kings? God is calling you this day. Come and receive life in abundance.

Remember that your mission here on earth is to spread the gospel of truth which is that, Jesus Christ is the Son of God and He died to set all free. All must repent from their sins and declare Jesus as Lord and Saviour in order to enter into the Kingdom of Heaven.

Matthew 20:28 says, "For even the Son of Man came not to be served but to serve others and to give his life as a ransom for many."

Go about spreading the gospel and draw all men unto Christ. Drink from the cup that never runs dry!

Devotional Twenty-Four

Fear Not!

¹²I know how to live on almost nothing or with everything. I have learned the secret of living in every situation, whether it is with a full stomach or empty, with plenty or little. ¹³For I can do everything through Christ, who gives me strength.

(Philippians 4:12-13 NLT)

Greetings to you my beloved family in Christ. A new day has come, and you are blessed to witness it. Thank God for this new day and ask for the grace to live according to His will bringing pleasure to His name.

What is that matter which causes you to fear? The Lord is saying Fear Not! On my prayer walk today, I came across a cat that scared me and caused me to shout hysterically. It later became a laughing topic, but the truth of the matter was that I was afraid of the cat.

What is it that causes you to fear? Rise above it today in prayer. Ask the Holy Spirit to open your eyes to see how great you are. For you are not a mistake but God's own creation created with a grand plan and purpose in mind. You are unique, beautifully and wonderfully made. Believe it and live like one who has a big God. Fear no evil for He is with you and lives in you.

Many live in bondage due to fear. You have remained in that place of work because you don't believe you are good enough. That's a lie! You have remained a victim of physical and emotional abuse because you don't believe you can do better. Another lie from the pit of hell. Why have you given room to fear? Rise in faith today!

Scripture says that after creation, God saw that all He created was good. You are a part of God's creation; one made a little lower than angels. You are marked out for greatness and this is the truth about you. You are created to be fruitful and multiply. Why then are you fearful of the unknown? You declare daily that you are the righteousness of God in Christ Jesus, yet you live in fear. Do you know who you are?

It is time you begin to see you the way God sees you. Discard every negative report you have received till date and open your eyes to see aright. As you draw near to God, He will reveal many things unto you about your identity. You are royalty because your Father is the King of the whole universe.

Reflect on your life thus far. What holds you down or stops you from achieving all that God desires for you? Open your eyes and see anew.

Rise up and occupy!

Devotional Twenty-Five

What is the Colour of Your Day?

¹³Nothing in all creation is hidden from God. Everything is naked and exposed before his eyes, and he is the one to whom we are accountable.

(Hebrews 4:13 NLT)

Every day is a blank canvas, you decide the design of each day. How colourful do you desire your day to be? Start painting with bright colours by filling your life with positive things. Quit engaging in negative thoughts or acts, instead, rise up knowing that God has given you dominion. Take charge and stop allowing your circumstances to dictate your day.

Genesis 1:26 KJV says, "And God said, Let us make man in our image, after our likeness: and let them have dominion over the fish of the sea, and over the fowl of the air, and over the cattle, and over all the earth, and over every creeping thing that creepeth upon the earth".

God has given you and I dominion over everything here on earth. Why have you allowed your situation to consume and overwhelm you? Rise up knowing that you have the power to create the world you want to see. If you are a child of the Most High God, you have the power to speak life and change your world. You cannot see change if you fail to speak life. Impossible!

Now is the time to create the world you want to see. You have all you need on the inside of you. Decide to live again and start living as God intended. What are you trusting God for today? Start thanking Him for the many blessings coming your way. Trust that He has handled every matter then rest in Him.

I choose to live an intentional life from this very minute. I choose to be happy and grateful this day. God has removed the scale from my eyes, I can see again! I will rejoice and be glad for I have been empowered to shine wherever I am placed.

You have the power to rejoice or remain sorrowful. We are all here on earth with a God-defined timeline. I choose to take charge by engaging with the Holy Spirit at all times. I will no longer trust in my own abilities but rely solely on the Spirit of God to lead and order my very steps. This way, I will always win and dominate as I should.

Finally, choose life and start living. Run to God and ask for mercy. All that you need has already been provided. Open your eyes and see the goodness all around you.

Devotional Twenty-Six

The Mystery of Life

¹⁰For we must all stand before Christ to be judged. We will each receive whatever we deserve for the good or evil we have done in this earthly body. ¹¹Because we understand our fearful responsibility to the Lord, we work hard to persuade others. God knows we are sincere, and I hope you know this, too.

(2 Corinthians 5:10-11 NLT)

Greetings to you my beloved family in Christ Jesus. Today's message is for all who are experiencing life with unanswered questions. Many ask why bad things happen to good people or why many have nothing whilst others live in abundance.

Solomon said in Ecclesiastes that "Life is meaningless". If this is so, why then do you worry or stress about matters around you. In fact, some work very hard but still end up poor whilst others work little hours and earn millions. This is the mystery of life that no one truly understands.

Bother yourself not about matters such as this instead live each day like it was your last ensuring that you give your very best. Thank God for your today and make the most of it. I am determined to make today count. This is my decision. What's yours?

If we are indeed like vapour or mere dust, why then do we waste our precious gifted time on matters that only promote heartache and unnecessary ailments? Can we truly live a life free from worries and heartache?

God is calling you and I back to His feet today. Yes, there will be issues that might cause you to fret or worry but you must decide to take it to God in prayer and leave it there. Philippians 4:6-7 says "Don't worry about anything; instead, pray about everything. Tell God what you need and thank him for all he has done. Then you will experience God's peace, which exceeds anything we can understand. His peace will guard your hearts and minds as you live in Christ Jesus."

If you truly desire the peace of God which surpasses all understanding to fill your heart, you must humble yourself and pray to God knowing that every matter presented to Him will be tended to at His own time. Yes, some matters might not be answered whilst some will. Only God truly knows why. Our uttermost focus must be to please the Father "God Almighty". For we are all here on an assignment. It's important to live a purposeful life for the end can come anytime. Therefore, make it your purpose to please the Father.

Devotional Twenty-Seven

Capture the Moment

¹⁷If I were doing this on my own initiative, I would deserve payment. But I have no choice, for God has given me this sacred trust. ¹⁸What then is my pay? It is the opportunity to preach the Good News without charging anyone. That's why I never demand my rights when I preach the Good News.

(1 Corinthians 9:17-18 NLT)

Greetings to you my blessed family in Christ Jesus. Where are you today? Rise up and give thanks unto God Most High. Giving up is no option instead be of good courage this day and trust again. Trust in God for He is too mighty to fail you.

What is it that God has planned for you? Cry unto God this day and ask Him to show it unto you. Jacob wrestled with God in Gen 32 saying "I will not leave you until you bless". There must come a time when you decide to remain in His presence until that matter is resolved. Many are trusting God for one thing or another but lack the grace to wait on Him. There is no one-time quick fix method with God. You must develop the act of waiting which requires the fruit of patience. Knock that door of mercy and don't leave until He opens it and blesses you.

The nature of man is to give up. Looking at the story of the Israelites who were freed from slavery and on their way to the promised land. Despite all that the Lord had done and was still doing, they easily gave up on God when faced with obstructions on the way. They moaned and complained along the way due to lack of faith and trust in God. Is this you today? It is time you decide to tarry in His presence regardless of how long or how hard the situation has been. Perseverance and persistence are required in this case. Trust in the Lord and keep trusting Him for He is able.

Finally, why do you serve God Almighty? Are you serving Him for bread alone? Are you with Him to truly serve Him whether He gives or not? It is time you lay aside every weight and face the King of Kings with a heart of gratitude. Lord, use me as you please dear Lord. For your glory, I will do anything. Can you say this? Can you make such statements?

God bless you as you stay fixed on Him. Capture the moment and dwell there. Stay with God in the place of worship. Dwell with Him for as long as it takes. The more you draw closer to God, the more He draws closer to you. Go deeper today and enjoy the abundance of His presence. His name is Jehovah!

Devotional Twenty-Eight

Set Boundaries

¹⁵For the despondent, every day brings trouble; for the happy heart, life is a continual feast. ¹⁷A bowl of vegetables with someone you love is better than steak with someone you hate.

(Proverbs 15:15, 17 NLT)

Greetings to you my beloved Family in Christ Jesus. A new day is here again, give thanks unto the Lord for His mercies endureth forever. Decide to make today count. Impact a life by sowing good seeds. Whatever you sow, you shall reap.

As I walked down the streets of Sutton Coldfield today, I approached an unfamiliar territory that seemed out of bound. This path had no pavements making it impossible to walk through, but I pressed on regardless and to my amazement, saw grand houses and mansions. I was astonished at the beauty before me. I never believed such existed in the United Kingdom.

There are set boundaries in our world today. This is the reality whether we believe it or not. The path I walked through today wasn't made for trespassers or commoners, but I walked through it regardless. I was determined to see beyond. If God says that Kings and Princes will come to your light, then you can no longer remain one with a beggar or slavery mentality. You must decide to rise up and begin to dream again.

It is time to revisit your vision board again. Ask the Holy Spirit to help re-define and re-create your vision according to God's plan. You must get tired of living a mediocre life. It is time to say, "Enough is Enough" and truly believe that the era of lack has come to an end. You must press on into the realm of abundance.

My prayer is that the good Lord will strengthen and cause you to rise up into that place of clarity and purpose. No more will you walk blindly or sow foolishly. You will begin to sow wisely and reap bountifully in Jesus mighty name Amen. You are part of the body of Christ and the best is reserved for you. Therefore, possess your possession and cease from accepting little. Fight every Spirit of lack and press into the era of victory and open heavens.

Devotional Twenty-Nine

Your Response

¹⁰So I am willing to endure anything if it will bring salvation and eternal glory in Christ Jesus to those God has chosen. ¹¹This is a trustworthy saying: If we die with him, we will also live with him.

(2 Timothy 1:10-11 NLT)

Greetings to you my blessed family in Christ Jesus. For Christ came to give you and I live in abundance. He died to set mankind free from the curse of sin. What a glorious God I serve? He is mighty and glorious in battle. Thank You, Lord!

What is your response to God today? Many assume they know Him. I repeat my question again - Are you truly saved? Are you truly free from sin? Many refuse to take heed to His voice. The Lord has been calling for your attention, but you keep deferring the call. You have chosen to turn a blind eye to His call. I ask you to obediently respond to Him before it's too late.

How long will you continue in your old ways? How long will you take matters into your own hands? How long will you go about spreading lies? You cannot claim to be saved when you are living a double life. God is calling you back to the place of Worship. For now, is the time to know Him. Waste no more time instead run to Him today with open arms.

For the Father awaits you at the gate. He has been waiting patiently for your return. Hosea 6:6 says "I want you to show love, not offer sacrifices. I want you to know me more than I want burnt offerings". For God is more interested in your heart than your tithes and offering. You cannot deceive or manipulate God with your money. He knows those who are His.

Return now that He is near. Seek His face now and turn from your wicked ways. Trust in Him completely and let Him transform you as He desires. You cannot continue living a lie "hot today and cold tomorrow". For the time has come to make a decision, it is either God or the devil. Make your choice now!

Can you honestly make this bold statement like Paul in 2 Corinthians 5:11 "Because we understand our fearful responsibility to the Lord, we work hard to persuade others, God knows we are sincere, and I hope you know this, too?"

It is important to fix your eyes on things above. You must choose to please the Father daily by dedicating your time to Him doing exactly what He demands.

Devotional Thirty

Make A Clean Slate with God

¹⁷Therefore, come out from among unbelievers, and separate yourselves from them, says the Lord. Don't touch their filthy things, and I will welcome you. ¹⁸And I will be your Father, and you will be my sons and daughters, says the Lord Almighty."

(2 Corinthians 6:17-18 NLT)

Greetings to you my blessed family in the Lord. Are you ready to discard your old way of thinking to allow the new to come in? Now has come the time to Rise above your so-called wisdom in order to let God fill you afresh. Let out the old wine for the new wine to come in.

Hurry gather all you can and let God fill you afresh. Cleansing is in progress but only a selected few will partake in this. Some might ask what I mean. I'm afraid to say that it is as simple as it reads. Only a selected few will truly allow God into their hearts to clean out every junk that lies on the inside of them. Lies which seem or look like the truth must all come out saith the Lord.

This question applies to both the young and the old. For none is exempted. God is asking you today, are you ready for change? Many would feel they are, but the truth is that they are not truly ready for change. They are not ready for the internal transformation because they believe they are right with God. Are you one that assumes all is perfect between you and God?

Go back to God and ask for help to see the true state of your heart. You must see in order to know the truth.

God is ready to break the ways of old. He is ready to break the barriers created by religion and culture. God is ready to transform and renew lives. Are you ready for Him? Are you ready to make a clean slate with God? Are you ready to discard the old in order to create room for the new?

Now is the time to humbly bow before God and ask for mercy. For God is rich in mercy and ready to bless all who are truly thirsty and aching for more of Him. Are you ready? God will not force you to do that which you are not prepared for. The choice is yours!

Do not answer God using your own intelligence instead ask the Holy Spirit to teach you the right way to commune with God.

Devotional Thirty-One

Who Is Your Go-To Person?

¹⁷Don't rejoice when your enemies fall; don't be happy when they stumble. ¹⁸For the Lord will be displeased with you and will turn his anger away from them. ¹⁹Don't fret because of evildoers; don't envy the wicked. ²⁰For evil people have no future; the light of the wicked will be snuffed out.

(Proverbs 24:17-20 NLT)

Greetings to you my blessed and favoured brothers and sisters in Christ. Today has come and you are privileged to witness it. Therefore, rejoice and be glad for it has pleased the Lord to grant you life in abundance. Celebrate for He is good and His mercies endureth forever.

Where are you positioned today? It is important to abide under the wings of the Almighty in order to enjoy the blessings available for the children of Zion. What has the Lord given you to do this season? Do it well with a heart of gratitude.

Who do you approach when faced with a challenging matter? Who is your go-to person? Many believe it is foolish consulting God over certain matters as they can't physically see Him. Is this you? Why do you go to man before consulting God? It is important to know that God is Alpha and Omega. None compares to Him. God must be your go-to person at every point in time if you truly want to experience victory in every area.

Practice makes perfect. Every matter that arises must be presented and dropped at the feet of God Almighty. It is important that you experience the abundance of the Lord in your life even before it is manifested for all to see. Faith is key!

Where is your mind today? I pray that your mind is focused on God alone. I pray that you will not follow the customs and ways of the world but be transformed daily by the renewal of your mind as you study the Word of God. It is important that you shine so bright wherever you are placed. You must begin to see yourself as God sees you. For you are not ordinary but one marked out for greatness. Therefore, start to see yourself in this light. Let there be light and there was light.

Finally, go to God in prayer over every matter that has caused unrest in your heart. Practise the act of remaining in God's presence for as long as it takes. Believe that God is with you in the storm and able to calm the wind. Be not afraid instead be of good courage. Rise up and serve Him obediently with a heart of gratitude. For the Lord watches over you, He never slumbers or sleeps. Rest in Him!

Devotional Thirty-Two

You Are Called to Serve

17This means that anyone who belongs to Christ has become a new person. The old life is gone; a new life has begun! 19For God was in Christ, reconciling the world to himself, no longer counting people's sins against them. And he gave us this wonderful message of reconciliation. 21For God made Christ, who never sinned, to be the offering for our sin, so that we could be made right with God through Christ.

(2 Corinthians 5:17, 19, 21 NLT)

Greetings to you my beloved brothers and sisters in Christ Jesus. A new day is before you because of the goodness and mercy of the Lord. Rise and give God the glory due to His name. For He is a Good Father!

Scripture says, "Think not of yourself higher than others". How do you treat others? Jesus served the disciples by bowing down to wash their feet. This was the lowest of levels, but He did it to teach you and I a valuable lesson. Quit your prideful act and serve others by loving and respecting them. You are called to serve!

It is important to step away from the trap of selfishness which is only interested in "me, myself and I". You cannot wander the face of the earth with a sense of entitlement. Your duty is to serve and love others regardless of their flaws. Your duty is to give and be a blessing unto others. You cannot wait to be loved before you love. Draw nearer to the Lord to know how best to please Him today.

Come out from amongst them saith the Lord. Who are you associated with and what fruits do they produce? How long will you live in pretence? You claim to be the influencer amongst your friends, but the truth is that they are influencing and changing your mindset daily. The more you hang around them, the more they rub off on you negatively. Beware!

Are you sold out for Jesus? Are you one willing to forsake all to please the Father? Are you ready to turn your back on your close and immediate family because of the call? How far are you willing to go with the lord? Selah.

The Father "Jehovah " is calling you and I back to Himself today. You are called to serve and not to be served. You are called to love and not demand love. Live to please the Father. Think not of yourself as higher than others, instead serve them as best as you can and remember that only a foolish man lives to please men. Live to please God and God alone.

Devotional Thirty-Three

Retention

¹⁷You may be asking why I changed my plan. Do you think I make my plans carelessly? Do you think I am like people of the world who say "Yes" when they really mean "No"? ²⁴But that does not mean we want to dominate you by telling you how to put your faith into practice. We want to work together with you so you will be full of joy, for it is by your own faith that you stand firm.

(2 Corinthians 1:17, 24 NLT)

Greetings to you my blessed family in Christ Jesus. Ephesians 4:17-18 says " So I tell you this, and insist on it in the Lord, that you must no longer live as the Gentiles do, in the futility of their thinking. They are darkened in their understanding and separated from the life of God because of the ignorance that is in them due to the hardening of their hearts". How long will you remain at that level? How long will you remain stuck due to the noise and distractions of life? What would it take to kickstart you to the next level? What are you doing about your Spiritual growth? Pause!

There is absolutely nothing tangible you can do on your own without the help and leading of the Holy Spirit. Therefore, cease from your labour and cling to the hem of His garment today. What business has darkness got to do with light? If you truly want to pass this test, you must refrain from your own ways and allow God into your space.

Engage not in unnecessary tasks that drain you spiritually, mentally and emotionally. Run to the throne room of grace and obtain mercy today. Receive new wine for the journey ahead for help is available. Drink as much as you need for the journey ahead now that you can. Defer not the time of action instead act now and enjoy the goodness thereof. Procrastinate no more!

Religion is enough to separate one from the promises of God. Culture is another therefore cease from following the traditions and customs of this world instead train yourself in the Lord by meditating on His Word daily and doing all He instructs you to do. It is important to master the true act of listening well to the Holy Spirit before acting. Rely not on your own understanding or strength instead trust in God for continuity and strength to finish the race well.

Dear Lord, I ask for strength to complete the race ahead of me. Help all who are desperately in need of change today and renew a right spirit within them. Holy Spirit fill all afresh for the journey ahead. Amen

Devotional Thirty-Four

Wrongful Assumptions

¹⁵For I am afraid that some of them have already gone astray and now follow Satan.

(1 Timothy 5:15 NLT)

Greetings to you my beloved family in Christ Jesus. A new day has come therefore rise up with a heart of gratitude. For it has pleased the Lord to bless you with life today. He alone is worthy to be praised. Hallelujah!

On the path of righteousness, it is important to rely not on assumptions, for it can cause you to fall or stumble. Run to the Holy Spirit for guidance so He can open your eyes to see and know the truth in order to be set free indeed.

Come forward now and assume the position given unto you by God today. Take on your position with every humility and reliance on God. Carefully follow the path laid before you by God and refrain from your old ways.

Run away from assumptions instead rely always on the Holy Spirit for clarity and assistance to fulfil purpose. 1 Timothy 4:7 says, "Have nothing to do with godless myths and old wives' tales; rather, train yourself to be godly." This can only be done by carefully observing the guidelines or instructions laid out by the Holy Spirit.

Pray at all times for the body of Christ and study the Word of God to show yourself approved. Run from doing things to impress men instead fear God and please Him. Your assignment is unto God and not man. Take note of this on your quest to running the race set before you and pleasing the Father.

God bless you as you do so. Have a blessed and fruitful day.

Devotional Thirty-Five

Look Forward

¹³No, dear brothers and sisters, I have not achieved it, but I focus on this one thing: Forgetting the past and looking forward to what lies ahead, ¹⁴I press on to reach the end of the race and receive the heavenly prize for which God, through Christ Jesus, is calling us.

(Philippians 3:13-14 NLT)

Greetings to you my blessed family in Christ Jesus. I am determined to press on regardless. What about you?

What are you determined to do? What is your next move? Many are so quick to act and slow to think. This is a wrong approach to doing anything of value. If you truly want to make a difference in the world, you must truly master the act of waiting upon the Lord.

No one likes waiting but waiting aright is key to your upliftment. You must trust God completely with no iota of doubt in your heart. That which He promised is exactly what He will do but as you wait, prepare for that which you are trusting Him for. Ask for the wisdom and grace to prepare aright and this will be given unto you.

If you are trusting God for the fruit of the womb, prepare by sowing seeds of fruitfulness and multiplication into your womb on a daily basis i.e., the Word of God. Speak it into your life and believe it. Take all that is necessary to assist your body throughout pregnancy. Take out time to rest and enjoy the ride as long as it takes. Difficult I know, but with the help of the Holy Spirit, you will succeed. Rejoice with those that rejoice and wait for your appointed time of manifestation.

Finally, what is God saying about that current situation? Take out time to know and understand what He is saying. Stop running ahead of God or taking matters into your hands. This only sets you back and causes you to fail miserably. Trust in the Lord and put no confidence in man. Develop a relationship with God. Spend time with Him and truly know Him.

God is able to do that which He promised but ensure you wait aright for the manifestation of His promise. God is still in the business of turning things around for your good. Believe!

Devotional Thirty-Six

A Bright New Day

¹³But Elijah said to her, "Don't be afraid! Go ahead and do just what you've said, but make a little bread for me first. Then use what's left to prepare a meal for yourself and your son. ¹⁴For this is what the Lord, the God of Israel, says: There will always be flour and olive oil left in your containers until the time when the Lord sends rain and the crops grow again!"

(1 Kings 17:13-14 NLT)

Judge not lest you will be judged by your Father in heaven. Can you honestly stand as one pure and blameless before the Lord? If not, stay far away from judging and condemning others. For the race ahead requires every seriousness, determination and perseverance to complete it. Quit worrying about the deed of others, focus on your race.

So, I found myself in a quiet spot yesterday. Unable to mingle with others but happy to spend time with my maker. Isn't this the place to be? I watched a movie about King Josiah, and this highlighted key truths about mankind. We have many decisions to make on earth, but the key decision lies in our salvation. You are either for God or the devil. You are either part of the kingdom of light or darkness. Where do you belong?

The time has come to make a decision. Not just any but the right decision. King Josiah decided to rise up and make a difference. He decided to destroy all other gods in order to lift up the name of Jehovah. For He raised up the banner of Jehovah in His time and pleased the Father. Are you able to stand boldly before the people to declare who Jesus is to you?

I remember a time in the Middle East when I was forced to sing in the open by my colleagues. Without thinking, the first and only song that came out of my mouth was unto the Lord "Hallelujah, you have won the victory". Immediately the staff approached me instructing me to stop because the song disturbed the people. Many couldn't stand the power behind the song and this caused trouble instantly. This was a night of joy for me because I lifted the name of Jesus out in the open.

There is more the Father requires of you and I. Are you ready to lift the banner of Jesus in your home, place of work etc.? Are you ready to trouble the waters to bring glory to the Father? Now is the time when the wheat will be separated from the chaff. Get ready!

Devotional Thirty-Seven

Crazy Faith

¹⁵Nor do we boast and claim credit for the work someone else has done. Instead, we hope that your faith will grow so that the boundaries of our work among you will be extended. ¹⁷As the Scriptures say, "If you want to boast, boast only about the Lord." ¹⁸When people commend themselves, it doesn't count for much. The important thing is for the Lord to commend them.

(2 Corinthians 10:15, 17-18 NLT)

Greetings to you my beloved family in Christ. Are you weary and tired of waiting? Receive strength today. Allow not the devil to steal away your joy and hope instead press forth into unending joy and gladness. For you will end well in Jesus mighty name Amen

The place of sorrow is truly the place of darkness therefore ensure you run far away from it. Many are sorrowful because of their current situation and world. Why are you sorrowful? Stand up today and assume your rightful position of faith. Remember that you are light, and your duty is to shine so bright for every hidden agenda to be revealed. Wherever you dwell, grace abounds.

My children perish for lack of knowledge. Many are running after the wrong things, many are chasing failed projects and broken dreams, many are running out of their place of rest because of fear and anxiety. God is saying to you today, come back into my place of safety. Come now that ye may truly know the way to go. Be anxious for nothing!

Ask for insight so that you may see aright. Ask for wisdom in order to move aright. For whatever you ask for, this you shall receive, if you remain in the place of trust and faith. You cannot ask with doubt in your heart. The call is for those who have crazy faith; those who are willing to stand out of the crowd in the place of faith whether people mock them or not. It doesn't matter what the doctor or experts say, what God says must be the pillar that holds your life and entire being.

Come out from their midst and believe God like never before. Trust Him to save your marriage, trust Him for a great job, trust Him for restoration of health and your mind. Trust Him even when your current view is obscured and blurry. Keep trusting, for God is still in the business of turning things around for your good. Just believe!

Step out today in faith and hold high the banner of Jesus Christ. For you serve a God that never fails. Turn away from the ways of old and step into the realm of faith today. Step into the will of the Father.

Devotional Thirty-Eight

Abundance

⁸And God will generously provide all you need. Then you will always have everything you need and plenty left over to share with others. ⁹As the Scriptures say, "They share freely and give generously to the poor. Their good deeds will be remembered forever." ¹⁰For God is the one who provides seed for the farmer and then bread to eat. In the same way, he will provide and increase your resources and then produce a great harvest of generosity in you. ¹¹Yes, you will be enriched in every way so that you can always be generous. And when we take your gifts to those who need them, they will thank God.

(2 Corinthians 9:8-11 NLT)

Greetings to you my blessed family in Christ Jesus. Determine in your heart to rejoice today and celebrate this new season. For I know that all things worketh together for the good of those who love the Lord. As long as you love and serve Yahweh, all things will work together for your good.

I don't care what has been or how it has been till date. I press forward, looking ahead and bringing forth life through my mouth. You have a choice to speak life or death over that situation. As for me, I choose to speak life. I will celebrate for the Lord is good and His mercies endureth forever. What about you?

So, the past months have been bitter-sweet, worry no more! He has a plan for your life and this you must treasure so much and abide in. Jeremiah 29:11 Message translation says "I know what I'm doing. I have it all planned out—plans to take care of you, not abandon you, plans to give you the future you hope for".

Therefore, determine in your heart to rest in His Word this season. GOD knows what He is doing. Even though I walk through the valley of the shadow of death, I will fear no evil for God is with me. This applies to you too. In that mess, God is there. In that bitter place, God is there. He is with you whether you see Him or not. He is right there with you. Call on Him today and embrace this divine moment with God, the Father.

Shout out His name today and rest in who He is...He is a good Father. Hallelujah

Devotional Thirty-Nine

Don't Get Tired

¹⁷Each of you should continue to live in whatever situation the Lord has placed you, and remain as you were when God first called you. This is my rule for all the churches.

(1 Corinthians 7:17 NLT)

Don't get tired of running the race set before you. Keep the momentum and run as fast as you can whilst you can. You will eventually complete the task set if you keep at it.

Do you occasionally get tired of pursuing your dreams or that God-driven task? I do. In fact, the truth is, I get tired of running but then again that still small voice puts things back into perspective for me saying "don't give up for there's so much to do for the Father". This voice kicks me back into motion and the race continues. What kicks you back into motion?

You see, many years ago I had a near-death experience that highlighted my purpose on earth. This was my rebirth stage which pushed me into God's plan. I have one purpose which is to worship my Father in Spirit and truth. To occupy and advance the Kingdom of Heaven. My job is so clear hence why I am driven to do as much as I do but we are not all the same. Therefore rest!

I have had many people come to me asking how I do what I do. I honestly don't know the answer. One thing I know is that God wouldn't give you or I more than we can chew. You are unique and so am I. It is time to know who you truly are and run your set race. The bible says in Proverbs 14:12 "There is a path before each person that seems right, but it ends in death".

My question for you today is "What path are you on?" Are you chasing after the wrong things and exhausted because of your many failed attempts? Isn't it time you reflect on your journey so far? As for me, I have decided to reflect on my life in order to finish well. I will succeed as long as I remain on the path laid out for me by God Almighty and not man. I have chosen to rely on God solely even if it's not understood by people around me. What about you?

Quit comparing yourself to others. Remain on your lane and be the very best you can be. What gifts do you have? Lay it all down and use it to your advantage. There is so much on the inside of you to give.

Devotional Forty

Get Back into Action!

¹⁷This means that anyone who belongs to Christ has become a new person. The old life is gone; a new life has begun!

(2 Corinthians 5:17 NLT)

So, you started with so much zeal and energy, why have you given up now? My brothers and sisters in Christ Jesus, determine in your heart to get back into action today regardless of the situation around you. "Rise up" has been the command throughout this season. This isn't because you are not already standing, No! It is because the level is rising daily, and it is important to keep climbing higher on this path of righteousness. You cannot afford to get tired or sit due to frustration and exhaustion. Rise and keep rising!

I decided to go for a walk today even though my body said otherwise. It is important to push forward in order to rise to the next level. Many times, force must be applied to that body in order to press forward into victory. You cannot win by laying down. You must stand up to press forward.

Wake up from that pitiful state of unbelief and fear. Determine in your heart to think only of positive things. Focus solely on God's promises and begin to imagine the impossible come forth. Speak what you want into existence. Speak and keep speaking!

Finally, execute Faith now and run far away from every trace of fear. Today, I arise in victory. I am a winner and so are you. I have spoken this, and I believe it. What about you? What are you speaking into your life and the lives of your children? Speak positive words and begin to see things move according to God's plan.

Song: I will not be silent; I will always worship you.

Go ahead and occupy the world you see. This is your only opportunity to create, therefore create the world you want to see and enjoy it. Live no more in pain and suffering. Rise out of fear today and assume the mind of Christ. Greater is He that is in you than he that is in the world. You must know who you are. Enjoy Now! Live your best life now! The choice is yours!

Devotional Forty-One

Stand Up and Do the Needful

17Each of you should continue to live in whatever situation the Lord has placed you, and remain as you were when God first called you. This is my rule for all the churches.

(1 Corinthians 7:17 NLT)

What is that which you know you must do but afraid to do? Get on with the task and quit living in fear or unbelief.

Greetings to you family in Christ Jesus. Today's message is aimed to awaken your Spirit man into action. Get on with it!

Get on with the task you planned to do. Get on with that business you planned to start. Stop living in fear. Quit allowing unbelief to rob you of your joy and possession. The real question is: who gave you the task to do? Was it God or man? If God instructed you to do anything, please do it now. If you planned to do it, ask for insight and move as led. Does this make sense?

The time has come to run away from procrastination. So, you have been sitting down on that idea for months, years and decades hoping to start that business but unsure of how to start. The time has come to run with the idea given to you by the Holy Spirit. Your Father created the whole universe therefore you have the ability and gift of creating too. Create the world you want to see.

I have longed to write books but struggled to start. Well, today is a new day and I am determined to rise regardless and do it by the grace and power of God. Faith without works is dead! If you are one sitting and waiting for an angel to appear before you move into action, you might remain there forever. Stand up!

The time has come to get on with it. What is the worst that could happen? Rejection! Worry not, instead move as led and watch God turn things around for your good. Do the course you planned to do. Just do it! And if you are one hiding behind affordability, there are many free courses online. Explore and start.

Wake up from your sleep and begin to act as instructed. For the Holy Spirit dwells on the inside of you and He is available to help you always. Hallelujah! Make use of what you have and quit living in fear or denial.

Now is the time!

Devotional Forty-Two

Despair!

¹¹So if the old way, which has been replaced, was glorious, how much more glorious is the new, which remains forever! ¹²Since this new way gives us such confidence; we can be very bold. ¹⁷For the Lord is the Spirit, and wherever the Spirit of the Lord is, there is freedom. ¹⁸So all of us who have had that veil removed can see and reflect the glory of the Lord. And the Lord—who is the Spirit—makes us more and more like him as we are changed into his glorious image.

(2 Corinthians 3:11-12, 17-18 NLT)

Greetings to you my blessed family in Christ Jesus. Give thanks to the Lord for He is good and His mercies endureth forever. Make a joyful noise o ye people, rejoice for the Lord made it possible for you and I to see a new day. Hallelujah

Are you tired of believing or almost at the borderline of giving up? Hang in there for help is on the way. The message today is short and direct. Lift up your hands and allow the Holy Spirit to lift you out of that place of despair. You cannot afford to give up on your dreams. No, you can't! Rise out of that pit now and move as directed.

Many have trusted but received no good news. Many have lost loved ones even though they prayed for them to rise out of the boat of sickness and disease. Hang in there! Yes, I know you have been let down by those you loved and respected, worry not for God has come to lift you out of that pit of sadness and self-pity. This is a new day, and you are alive to witness it. Rejoice!

Rejoice even when all you see looks depressing and overwhelming. Rejoice because God has the final say not you. Rejoice because Christ died for you and intercedes for you. Rejoice because you are not alone. Greater is He that is in you than He that is in the World. Rejoice because help has come to save you. All that's required today is BELIEVE.

You must believe that Help is here and that you are not alone. The Holy Spirit will help you out of that pit. Have faith that the Most High God will not fail you. Rise today and rejoice!

He has a plan for you and it is good. This plan should be the source of your joy and gladness today. His plan is good!

Devotional Forty-Three

Ask for Help

¹¹Furthermore, because we are united with Christ, we have received an inheritance from God, for he chose us in advance, and he makes everything work out according to his plan. ¹³And now you Gentiles have also heard the truth, the Good News that God saves you. And when you believed in Christ, he identified you as his own by giving you the Holy Spirit, whom he promised long ago. ¹⁴The Spirit is God's guarantee that he will give us the inheritance he promised and that he has purchased us to be his own people. He did this so we would praise and glorify him.

(Ephesians 1:11, 13-14 NLT)

For the thief cometh to steal, kill and destroy but Jesus came to give life to those who are in need. Are you in need today?

Are you ready to own up to the fact that you just don't know what else to do? Are you ready to admit that your life is falling apart, and you need God's help? Are you ready to admit that you need help raising your children or that you need help waiting on the Lord to bless you with the fruit of the womb? Are you ready to admit that you are in need?

Many find it hard to ask for help. I remember a friend offering to sow a seed into my life which I found hard to receive. I asked God for help but found it hard to receive from those He blessed to bless me. I never knew it was a problem until it presented itself to me. Are you one who loves to give but struggles to receive? Ask for help today.

Over the years, God has taught me to gradually slow down by drawing me unto Himself. I was like Martha running here and there trying to sort out every matter. Without God, it is impossible to do anything worthwhile. Without the Holy Spirit, it's impossible to move aright. Without faith, it is impossible to please God. Be persistent in prayer and trust God for all things. This is one of the secrets to finishing well.

Life will not always make sense or run smoothly as planned. No! In fact, on this journey of life, there are many hurdles and mountains to climb. Without God on your side, it is impossible to succeed therefore call on the Holy Spirit today and ask for help. Ask until your request becomes your reality.

"Thy Kingdom come; thy will be done on earth as it is done in heaven." God's kingdom will come over every situation presented at His feet today meaning He will make a way for all matters. His will be done in your life and mine in Jesus mighty name Amen.

Ask and keep asking. Don't give up until what you've asked for becomes your reality. His will be done on Earth as it is done in Heaven. Rest in Him!

Devotional Forty-Four

Understanding

¹³He shot his arrows deep into my heart. ²¹Yet I still dare to hope when I remember this: ²²The faithful love of the Lord never ends! His mercies never cease. ²³Great is his faithfulness; his mercies begin afresh each morning. ²⁴I say to myself, "The Lord is my inheritance; therefore, I will hope in him!" ²⁵The Lord is good to those who depend on him, to those who search for him. ²⁶So it is good to wait quietly for salvation from the Lord. ²⁷And it is good for people to submit at an early age to the yoke of his discipline: ³¹For no one is abandoned by the Lord forever.

(Lamentation 3:13, 21-27, 31 NLT)

You have the power to create the world you desire. Do you believe this?

Greetings to you my beloved family in Christ Jesus. In the faith, many believers claim to know God but struggle to believe His Word. Yes, many know the bible inside/out but how many truly understand the bible?

"And He said, to you it has been given to know the mysteries of the kingdom of God, but to the rest, it is given in parables, that 'Seeing they may not see, and hearing they may not understand" Luke 8:10.

It is impossible to know the mysteries of God without the help of the Holy Spirit. You can decide to study the bible from now till eternity but without the Holy Spirit, you wouldn't see or understand the secrets in the Word. Therefore, note that Spiritual insight is key on this path of salvation.

Quit relying on your own strength or abilities instead learn to ask the Holy Spirit for help. You are where you are today because God permitted it to be so. For nothing happens by chance therefore, trust and rely solely on Him.

Listen carefully for direction then move obediently. Quit running blindly instead kick start your faith by putting it into action. Don't just say a thing, begin to "act" accordingly as instructed by the Holy Spirit.

Have Faith!

Devotional Forty-Five

Seasons

²"Everything is meaningless," says the Teacher, "completely meaningless!" ⁵The sun rises and the sun sets, then hurries around to rise again. ¹⁸The greater my wisdom, the greater my grief. To increase knowledge only increases sorrow.

(Ecclesiastes 1:2, 5, 18 NLT)

Greetings to you my family in Christ Jesus. What motivates you? What inspires you or encourages you to do that which you do? Selah

Many work hard to feed their pressing needs. They work round the clock with no time to spare. They complain and ask for a break but are unable to rest because they have very little to survive on. Is this you? Are you tired of complaining?

Have you ever wondered how the poor or needy survive? I remember one of the "feed the homeless projects" carried out in December 2019, one of the guys who collected a food bag from me decided to hang around with the crew to pray and help out. After the short prayer, I approached him and asked how He was doing. To my amazement, he replied saying "He was great and had learned to quit complaining but remain thankful to God at all times. He said he was helping out because he was dreading returning to his temporary accommodation which wasn't nice at all with bad tenants who used drugs. He had nothing, yet he was thankful. He didn't know what He would eat on a daily basis but believed that God would provide for him. This man was in great need but chose to trust God.

The summary of today's message is: Thank God for your present situation whether bad or good. Thank God regardless of how heavy your cross is to carry. I was reminded again today by the Holy Spirit to lay aside my own problems and tend to the Father's business. We have all been given assignments to do by God. Yes, it might not seem like the right time to move but you must move as led by the Holy Spirit. Quit waiting for the season to look favourable. When He says move, just move!

Obedience is better than sacrifice. You have the ability to do that which God has given you to do because He dwells on the inside of you, and He has made all things accessible and available unto you. You must trust God and not your ability. Be bold and be strong for the Lord your God is with you. Take back all that's been given unto you and run with it.

Devotional Forty-Six

Endurance

⁶For God, who said, "Let there be light in the darkness," has made this light shine in our hearts so we could know the glory of God that is seen in the face of Jesus Christ. ⁷We now have this light shining in our hearts, but we ourselves are like fragile clay jars containing this great treasure. This makes it clear that our great power is from God, not from ourselves.

(2 Corinthians 4:6-7 NLT)

Greetings to you my brothers and sisters in Christ Jesus. Are you able to endure the race set before you?

Many are living with no sense of purpose. Are you impatient and unable to focus on a task till completion? Are you good at starting but bad at completing tasks? Now is the time to ask the Holy Spirit for the gift of endurance.

As a child of the Most High God, all that you require to finish the race has been given unto you. This means that all you need is with you and that project will be completed as long as you set your eyes on Jesus Christ. Allow the Holy Spirit to show you the way to go. You must humble yourself to pray, seek His face and then turn from your wicked ways.

It's important to note that relying on your understanding will not get you to the finish line. You must learn to trust God like never before. The Lord is calling for your undivided attention.

Now is the time to run the race set before you and keep running until you get to the finish line.

Allow the Holy Spirit to lead you on the path of acceleration and comfort. Allow the Holy Spirit to order your steps into higher grounds. Surrender and move as led.

Proverbs 10:17 says "He who learns from instruction and correction is on the [right] path of life [and for others his example is a path toward wisdom and blessing], But he who ignores and refuses correction goes off course [and for others his example is a path toward sin and ruin]".

Come closer to God today and receive the grace to run and keep running. New grace is available for those who need it. New strength is available now so run to the throne room of mercy and receive all available today.

Song: Fill my cup Lord I lift it up, Lord

Have a blessed and Spirit-filled day.

Devotional Forty-Seven

Stop Shouting

¹²We can say with confidence and a clear conscience that we have lived with a God-given holiness[c] and sincerity in all our dealings. We have depended on God's grace, not on our own human wisdom. That is how we have conducted ourselves before the world, and especially toward you. ¹³Our letters have been straightforward, and there is nothing written between the lines and nothing you can't understand. I hope someday you will fully understand us

(2 Corinthians 1:12-13 NLT)

Greetings to you my blessed family in Christ Jesus. My message changed suddenly after a deep sleep. Read carefully!

Do you value those you have? Do you value your parents/husband/wife/children/close relatives? Value those who are alive now that you can, so that you would not regret your actions later. This dream hit me so hard in fact, I woke up minutes ago feeling bad but thank God for the wake-up call.

The time has come to value those around you by showing how much you love them. Spend quality time with your parents, family etc. and quit making excuses. Thank God for their presence in your life and stop complaining. As I was about to go to bed yesterday, my mum asked to pray with me, but my first reaction spoke louder than the latter. I didn't want to pray in fact, I wanted to sleep but she was persistent, and we prayed. The prayer was all about my siblings and I. Amazing love!

My message today might be hard to chew for many who reads it, but it is the truth, and it is here to set you free. Make out time to call those you call family. Quit complaining and moaning instead see the joy in having them around. Many would kill to have what you have. Husbands, value that wife who has spent her years looking after you and the children. Wives, value that man regardless of his wrongs and many mistakes. Children, value your parents now that they are alive and parents, value your children by spending quality time with them as best as you can. Make out time for those you love now.

To those who cheat on their loved ones, now is the time to mend your ways. For Jesus is coming sooner than you think. Turn from your wicked ways and love as commanded by God.

Are you tired of running that race set before you? Why not ask the Holy Spirit for help today? Ask for the grace to love those who don't value or show you, love. If you truly want to be a disciple of Christ Jesus, you must carry your cross and follow Him. It doesn't matter how heavy the cross is, keep moving! Keep praying! Keep pressing forward! For He would send help at the appointed time. You are not alone!

Devotional Forty-Eight

God Is So Good

¹⁷For our present troubles are small and won't last very long. Yet they produce for us a glory that vastly outweighs them and will last forever! ¹⁸So we don't look at the troubles we can see now; rather, we fix our gaze on things that cannot be seen. For the things we see now will soon be gone, but the things we cannot see will last forever.

(2 Corinthians 4:17-18 NLT)

Greetings to you my blessed family in Christ Jesus. In as much as we like ensuring all things are in order, it is important to rest. Rest knowing that God is working things out for your good.

So, the morning came, and He woke me up. I was distracted again by my surroundings, so I decided to go for my morning walk even though it was raining because I knew I needed to speak to Him (the Holy Spirit). I needed to pray so I decided to see the goodness in the rain. God's goodness filled me as I walked and talked to Him. The rain was a blessing to me. I saw the goodness in the rain.

What do you see? What is your reality? Try your very best to see God's goodness in that situation. Are you job hunting or idle? Why not maximise the time you have by spending quality time with God instead of complaining and crying? There's so much you can do with the time given to you freely. The truth is that the time you have is a gift. Many lay in the graveyard unable to move because time has ended for them. You have time on your hands, and it is a gift therefore use it wisely. Pray for Christians everywhere, study the Word, make calls to friends and family, do free courses etc. Ask the Holy Spirit for insight and this will be given unto you. Move as directed!

Rest from your worries and see the beauty of God all around you. As for me, I have decided to rest. In fact, I have decided to make today count. Yes, I will! That situation will all make sense eventually. Surround yourself with wise people in the faith. Act thoughtfully and not carelessly. Bless others by putting a smile on their faces and allow God to handle your matter. He is able!

Rejoice I say rejoice! Rise up for the Lord is good and His mercies endureth forever. Hallelujah!

Devotional Forty-Nine

Carefully Study Your Actions!

¹⁷Starting a quarrel is like opening a floodgate, so stop before a dispute breaks out.

(Proverbs 17:14 NLT)

Greetings to you my Family in Christ. Today's devotional is written to get your undivided attention. My prayer is that all who receives this Word would see the light and work in it.

Carefully determine what pleases the Lord and do it. You cannot assume you are right with God because of your works or title. Engage with the Holy Spirit to see the true state of your heart. Are you led by your desires, feelings or will? If so, you are not where you ought to be. Turn from your ways now and allow Christ to transform you anew. You must understand that Jesus Christ is Lord and must remain Lord over your life at all times.

Jesus endured the pain of the cross for you to receive life in abundance. He submitted completely to God's will even though He was distressed. What about you? How do you live and conduct your life? Are you one who lives under your own light meaning you submit to no one but yourself? Carefully analyse your ways now and return to the lord before it is too late.

Are you one who allows anger and unforgiveness to control you? Remember that anger gives room for the devil. You must throw away your old ways and conform to the new nature governed and controlled by God Almighty. Surrender!

"Oh, that we might know the Lord! Let us press on to know him. He will respond to us as surely as the arrival of dawn or the coming of rains in early spring." "O Israel and Judah, what should I do with you?" asks the Lord. "For your love vanishes like the morning mist and disappears like dew in the sunlight. I want you to show love, not offer sacrifices. I want you to know me more than I want burnt offerings." Hosea 6:3-4, 6 NLT

Deep calleth unto deep. Do you hear His call? Rise up and draw closer to God Almighty.

Have a restful sleep and remain joyful in God...

Devotional Fifty

Your Position

¹⁰Carefully determine what pleases the Lord. ¹⁵So be careful how you live. Don't live like fools, but like those who are wise. ¹⁶Make the most of every opportunity in these evil days.

(Ephesians 5:10, 15-16 NLT)

Greetings to you my brothers and sisters in Christ Jesus. How many things are you doing this season? Yes, I understand that these are trying times for everyone however, you need to ensure you are where God wants you now. You can't be everywhere when He needs your attention. Now is the time to tune in to His voice that you may know the way to go.

Be anxious for nothing!

Are you one who complains about everything or are you having a mental breakdown because of the current uncertainties and economic situation? Calm yourself down and draw from the throne room of grace today.

Many would ask how one can rest in the storm. This I ask the Holy Spirit on a daily basis but one thing He says is that it is important to trust the one you claim you know. If indeed you are a child of God, you should make a decision to go home. Where is home? A home is a place of safety which is under God's wings. Abide in Him that He abides in you.

I have realised that all the Father wants is a relationship with His children. Christ has paid the price for you and I to approach the Father with no limitations. Why then do you allow the enemy to hold you back. You must consciously discard the noise in order to draw closer to the King of Kings.

I see the enemy working so hard to discourage the body of Christ this season, but all we need to do is run closer to God. Run to the place of safety. Run to the feet of Jesus Christ. It is important to draw strength from within you. For the power lies within. Worry not about the noise instead press forward regardless. This is possible if you are determined to work with the Holy Spirit. Without the Holy Spirit, it is impossible to approach the throne room of grace.

Spiritual discipline is key! Fix your eyes on Jesus and try to keep your eyes on Him as long as you can. Ask for the grace to sit at His feet. The call is for those who long to commune with their Father. He is waiting for you. Turn off the noise and draw closer to God today.

Devotional Fifty-One

Faith

⁶And it is impossible to please God without faith. Anyone who wants to come to him must believe that God exists and that he rewards those who sincerely seek him.

(Hebrews 11:6 NLT)

Greetings unto you my beloved family in Christ Jesus. How big is your faith? Though the world declares words contrary to God's Word, are you able to keep trusting and hoping for greater heights? The choice is yours!

I don't know about you, but I choose to trust in God more than ever before. For He giveth unto those He loves new life if they believe. Whose report do you believe? You have the power to believe that which you are being told today or not. The choice is yours! I have made up my mind to go God's way for the rest of my life. O that my eyes remain fixed on Him till He returns and takes me home. This is my posture. What about you?

There are many decisions one can make. You have a chance to paint the future you choose to see by executing faith. Now the mistake many make is not putting their faith into action. You say you believe but you don't work on it. Ask and it shall be given unto you saith the Lord.

James 1:6 says " But let him ask in faith, with no doubting, for he who doubts is like a wave of the sea driven and tossed by the wind.

You have the power to create and innovate. Get on with it! Begin to create the world you want to see by seeing it first in the Spirit. Speak it forth and await the appointed time of manifestation. For it shall surely come to pass

Finally, Hebrews 11:1says "Now faith is the assurance (title deed, confirmation) of things hoped for (divinely guaranteed), and the evidence of things not seen [the conviction of their reality—faith comprehends as fact what cannot be experienced by the physical senses]" AMP.

Have a blessed and fulfilled day.

Devotional Fifty-Two

Knowledge is Power

¹⁰Don't you believe that I am in the Father and the Father is in me? The words I speak are not my own, but my Father who lives in me does his work through me. ¹¹Just believe that I am in the Father and the Father is in me. Or at least believe because of the work you have seen me do.

(John 14:10-11 NLT)

Greetings to you my family in Christ Jesus. Who do you belong to? Have you ever asked yourself this question? Who are you and what is your identity? The answer to these questions can be found in the Father.

It is important to conduct yourself according to Heaven's standard. You cannot be transformed and remain as the old. It is impossible. When God steps in, all things change around you. A 360-degree makeover is guaranteed.

I am waiting at the gate for my children to return home saith the Father. Many would assume they are His and know how best to please Him, but the truth is that you cannot live in the realm of assumption or guesswork. You need to know the truth in order to be set free indeed.

Hosea 6:3, 6 NLT says "Oh, that we might know the Lord! Let us press on to know him. He will respond to us as surely as the arrival of dawn or the coming of rains in early spring." I want you to show love, not offer sacrifices. I want you to know me more than I want burnt offerings."

Total submission is key to receiving all that God has purposed for you. You can no longer exist like those of this world. For knowledge is power. You must engage with the Holy Spirit in order to know the way to go. He counsels and shows one the way to go if you admit that you are in need of His help.

Now is the time to run to the feet of the Master. Who is your Lord and Master? Reflect on this today. Who truly determines your destiny? You or God? The choice is yours. Remember that you are here on earth because He planned it to be so. Therefore, live no longer in your own light instead come under His light and let Him show you the way to go.

Take heed lest you fall!

Devotional Fifty-Three

Decisions Made

⁶Don't worry about anything; instead, pray about everything. Tell God what you need, and thank him for all he has done. ⁷Then you will experience God's peace, which exceeds anything we can understand. His peace will guard your hearts and minds as you live in Christ Jesus.

(Philippians 4:6-7 NLT)

Greetings to you my beloved family in Christ Jesus. You have the freedom to live life the way you desire. God has given you the freedom to decide what path you choose to take. You have the power to walk in His marvellous light or walk according to the will of the devil. The choice is yours. What decisions have you made?

Many cry out to God for help after making bad decisions contrary to His will. They cry out for mercy knowing fully well that they got themselves into that mess. God is rich in mercy and ready to help all who call unto Him, but it is important to make the right decisions by yielding to the Lordship of Jesus Christ. Carefully determine what pleases God then do it.

Are you tired of toiling that same mountain? Are you now ready to surrender to His will and accept Him as your Lord and Saviour? You see, the truth of the matter is that you must first come to your senses by owning up to your mistakes and asking for help. Ask for forgiveness and He will wipe away every stain from your garment. He will give you a brand-new robe and change your name. Approach His gate with a heart of gratitude, thank Him for all He has done for you and accept Jesus as your Lord and Saviour. The truth of the matter is that the Father longs for your undivided attention and loves you regardless of the path you choose to take. He cares about you and loves you unconditionally.

To abide under His wings is for your benefit. Choosing to submit under His lordship is for your protection. For under His wings lies everlasting joy and safety. What more do you want? Resting in God requires trust and Faith. You must decide to lean on the only rock that never fails. This is where you ought to be.

If you are happy running from pillar to post, go ahead and live as always but trust me when I say there's no better place to be than in the arms of the Father. It is better to trust in the Lord than to put your confidence in men.

Arise now and make the right decisions. Submit and allow Him to direct you accordingly.

Devotional Fifty-Four

He Is More Than Able

¹¹Furthermore, because we are united with Christ, we have received an inheritance from God, for he chose us in advance, and he makes everything work out according to his plan. ¹²God's purpose was that we Jews who were the first to trust in Christ would bring praise and glory to God. ¹³And now you Gentiles have also heard the truth, the Good News that God saves you. And when you believed in Christ, he identified you as his own by giving you the Holy Spirit, whom he promised long ago. ¹⁴The Spirit is God's guarantee that he will give us the inheritance he promised and that he has purchased us to be his own people. He did this so we would praise and glorify him.

(Ephesians 1:11-14 NLT)

Greetings to you my blessed family in Christ Jesus. God is more than able to change that situation, do you believe?

As I drove home today, I looked at the sky and saw the beauty of God. The birds of the air and fish of the sea, worry not about food and the Lord supplies their needs. Why then are you worried about tomorrow?

What is the worst that could happen? Are you worried that many would mock you? Stand knowing that the God you serve will never disappoint or fail you. Trust that He will make provision for you and cause you to smile like never before. It pays to put your confidence and trust in God and God alone.

Now is the time to lay down your petition before God and believe in your heart that He will handle all matters. Worship Him with all your might knowing that He has changed your situation for good.

God is ever ready to take the stage in your life. Give Him the key to your life by surrendering all to Him and allow Him to steer you in the right direction leading you unto higher grounds. Now is the time!

Trust God with all your heart and do not allow any doubt or fear into your heart. He is more than able to change your very situation for good. Do you believe?

Devotional Fifty-Five

Engagement

[11]I have observed something else under the sun. The fastest runner doesn't always win the race, and the strongest warrior doesn't always win the battle. The wise sometimes go hungry, and the skilful are not necessarily wealthy. And those who are educated don't always lead successful lives. It is all decided by chance, by being in the right place at the right time.

(Ecclesiastes 9:11 NLT)

Greetings to you my blessed family in Christ Jesus. Who are you engaged to? Who are you in partnership with, God or the devil?

Many are under the leadership of the devil unknowingly. So, your friend/partner betrayed you and you have decided never to forgive them. What does this mean? Well, you have accepted unforgiveness and hatred into your life giving room for the devil.

The truth is you cannot be for God and harbour unforgiveness or any form of sin in your heart. No! Sin has no place in the Kingdom of God. The Kingdom of Heaven has only one King who is God Almighty. In Him lies Jesus Christ the Son and the Holy Spirit. They are all one in all (Holy Trinity) therefore, when God says sin cannot be found in Him this means sin is not tolerated in His Kingdom.

Therefore, I beseech you my brothers and sisters in Christ to patiently examine your heart this day to determine what kingdom you belong to. By their fruits, you shall know them. I repeat my earlier statement " Many belong to the kingdom of darkness unknowingly". Turn from your wicked ways and realign back under the leadership of the Holy Spirit.

Now is the time to monitor the state of your garment ensuring that there are no stains on it. Take it upon yourself to wash that garment by stepping into the office of the Holy Spirit. Ask Him for help and He will truly guide and show you the way to go.

Revelations 22: 14-16 NIV says, "Blessed are those who wash their robes, that they may have the right to the tree of life and may go through the gates into the city. Outside are the dogs, those who practice magic arts, the sexually immoral, the murderers, the idolaters and everyone who loves and practices falsehood".

For it is not by power or might but by the Spirit of God who will open your eyes to see aright. Now is the time to connect to the one true God who knows you by name. He awaits you.

Devotional Fifty-Six

The Noise is deafening

⁵Let everyone see that you are considerate in all you do. Remember, the Lord is coming soon.

(Philippians 4:5 NLT)

Greetings to you my family in Christ Jesus. I have been on a journey for a few days and extremely occupied with tasks. How do you silence the noise in the midst of your busy schedule?

Many ask whether it is possible to hear God in the midst of chaos. My answer is yes you can. Make a conscious effort to silence the noise in your heart by focusing on Jesus Christ. Give Him your undivided attention for as long as you can. If 20 mins is what you have, give it to Him. You can't afford to be separated from Him now.

Join me in praising the Most High God. Drop all you are doing and praise Him as best as you can. For it pleased the Lord to spare your life in the midst of the storm, be of a cheerful heart.

A happy heart is good medicine, and a joyful mind causes healing, but a broken spirit dries up the bones. Proverbs 17:22 AMP

God bless you as you do so!

Devotional Fifty-Seven

How Big is Your Dream?

¹⁶I pray that from his glorious, unlimited resources he will empower you with inner strength through his Spirit. ¹⁷Then Christ will make his home in your hearts as you trust in him. Your roots will grow down into God's love and keep you strong.

(Ephesians 3:16-17 NLT)

Greetings to you my brothers and sisters in Christ Jesus. New life has been given unto all who believe. Receive all that the Lord places in your hands this day and make a joyful noise unto His name.

How big is your dream? Is your dream big enough to scare you? If it doesn't scare you, dream again. It is time to stretch your faith. Dig deeper and begin to dream like never before.

You must first see it, before you can receive it. Speak it forth and live your dream. For it is impossible to please God without faith. Have faith in Him!

Do you ever wonder why things are not going your way or as planned? It is time to draw closer to God so that He will reveal secrets unto you. It is time to let go of your old ways for God to take over your entire life.

Surrender all to Him and allow the Most High God redirect your steps as He originally planned. Open your eyes and begin to dream again. For your Father is the God of the whole universe. Jehovah is His name. He is too faithful to fail you.

What He says He would do is exactly what He will do. Fear not instead move in faith and believe like never before. Now is the time!

Devotional Fifty-Eight

What Do You Have?

¹¹Just believe that I am in the Father and the Father is in me. Or at least believe because of the work you have seen me do. ¹²"I tell you the truth, anyone who believes in me will do the same works I have done, and even greater works, because I am going to be with the Father. ¹³You can ask for anything in my name, and I will do it so that the Son can bring glory to the Father. ¹⁴Yes, ask me for anything in my name, and I will do it!

(John 14:11-14 NLT)

Greetings to you my beloved family in Christ Jesus. What are doing to improve yourself? Yes, today is about you.

What are you doing with the precious time given to you now? Are you trusting God for multiple streams of income? Can you honestly say you have exhausted all possible options of making extra money? This is the time to look within and use what you have.

What do you have? Bring it forward for multiplication to manifest. What is it you do well? Are you one who loves baking, cooking, sewing, ironing, dancing ? Do you have a lot of random goods in your home like me? Start with the little and allow God to do the multiplication.

For Jesus to feed the 5000 and more, He needed something to work with and that was the "Two fish and 5 loaves". He presented this before the Father and blessed it. The result was mind-blowing. He fed them all until they were full and had 12 baskets full of leftovers. This is what God can do and more.

Quit looking down on the small you have instead, start working with that small in order for increase to come. I realised I had some random goods in my garage which were brand-new and untouched. I posted them on eBay and the rest is history. Just like that, I have almost sold all items in 2 weeks. This was just a little idea given to me by the Holy Spirit. I could have disregarded it, but I didn't. What do you have at home, bring them forward and move as instructed? Start moving!

Now is the time to quit complaining and murmuring instead put your little ideas into action. There must be something you can do. Start now and wait expectantly for the Lord to bless you in abundance. You are unique and not of this world. Remember!

Do you remember the parable of the talents in Matthew 25. Meditate on this passage and ask the Lord to open your eyes to see that which He has given unto you so that you multiply it before His return. God bless you as you do so.

Devotional Fifty-Nine

Time Is Ticking!

¹⁰God's purpose in all this was to use the church to display his wisdom in its rich variety to all the unseen rulers and authorities in the heavenly places. ¹¹This was his eternal plan, which he carried out through Christ Jesus our Lord. ¹²Because of Christ and our faith in him, we can now come boldly and confidently into God's presence.

(Ephesians 3:10-12 NLT)

Greetings to you my brothers and sisters in Christ. Time is ticking and it is important that you pay close attention to what you do with the time given to you. How do you spend the precious time given to you? This is one to reflect upon.

I went out for my morning walk with a friend and was led on a detour leading me to another sister's house. It was important to obey the Holy Spirit even though it was not convenient or comfortable to change our route, but we did as instructed. Why? God has a set task for a set time and working in alignment with the Holy Spirit means you must adhere to every instruction given at that very hour received. You cannot defer or procrastinate if you are truly an obedient child of the Most High God.

Imagine sending a servant on an errand but he/she decides to ignore your instruction and go when it is convenient for them. What would you label the servant as? Disobedient. This is exactly how it works in the Kingdom of Heaven. God is the one and only true King, when He instructs, we must move accordingly however He would not force Himself on us. The rule of the Kingdom is to first believe that you are His and that He is yours then obediently follow His commands living to please Him alone through the help and leading of the Holy Spirit.

Today, many live following their own desires and decisions. They omit the permission of the King expecting that He would move on their say so. God is no slave to humans therefore you must carefully determine what pleases the Lord at all times then move as instructed. You cannot be a part of a kingdom without knowing the voice of the King. In this Kingdom, God made Christ an authority over the church i.e., you & I. Therefore, there is nothing we do without the permission of Jesus Christ. We do it all in the name of Jesus Christ. We have access to the throne room through Jesus Christ. This is the reality and truth of the Kingdom.

Finally, quit making excuses. Spend quality time with the Father now that He is near. Jehovah is calling!

Devotional Sixty

Who or What Inspires You?

⁹Honor the Lord with your wealth and with the best part of everything you produce. ¹⁰Then he will fill your barns with grain, and your vats will overflow with good wine. ¹³Joyful is the person who finds wisdom, the one who gains understanding.

(Proverbs 3:9-10, 13 NLT)

Greetings to you my beloved family in Christ Jesus. What is the state of your heart today? I woke up feeling exhausted and overwhelmed. I laid down on my bed wondering why I didn't feel happy. Is this how you feel today?

I am here to encourage you today. Weeping may endure for a night but joy cometh in the morning. Yes, I know you have been trusting God for change for some time now, but it is important you keep trusting. Find strength in His Word today. He is able!

God is able and He is still in the business of turning things around for your good. Now is the time to hold firm to the faith you profess. I know that my tomorrow will be great therefore I choose to rejoice today. What about you?

Let your day count. Make a decision to keep trusting God. Worship Him like never before. Choose to engage with Him by thanking Him for all He has done. There is nothing He cannot do therefore rest in Him.

Rejoice for He permitted your existence for a reason. It's not over until God says it's over. O rejoice today my friend for the Great High priest is mighty to save you. He is more than able! Yes, He is.

Meditate on His promises and wait for the appointed time of manifestation. It will surely come. I know it will.

Devotional Sixty-One

Abide!

¹⁵So be careful how you live. Don't live like fools, but like those who are wise. ¹⁶Make the most of every opportunity in these evil days. ¹⁷Don't act thoughtlessly, but understand what the Lord wants you to do.

(Ephesians 5:15-17 NLT)

Greetings to you my beloved brothers and sisters in Christ Jesus. Today's word is to shine light in your hearts opening you to greater secrets. Now is the time to know the truth in order to be set free.

"Even when I walk through the darkest valley, I will not be afraid, for you are close beside me. Your rod and your staff protect and comfort me. Psalms 23:4 NLT"

God's rod and staff are to keep you aligned and guided on the path of righteousness. Studying the Word releases you from entanglements and the lies of the enemy. His Word bringeth light and giveth stability to remain standing in this dark world. Many perish because of lack of knowledge. How long will you hide behind unstable rocks? Now is the time to know your God in order to remain secure forever.

Abide in God that He may abide in you. Even in the midst of the storm, you must continually declare His Word believing it will surely come to pass. I don't know about you but as for me, there is no alternative. It's God or nothing therefore I must get it right and keep at it as best as I can with the help of the Holy Spirit.

Run from negativity and falsehood. Learn to abide with your maker by regularly communing with Him. He is your father, and you are His children therefore talk to Him sincerely and don't leave unless He blesses you. Abide that He may abide in you.

In comparison with Martha, Mary knew her place which was at the feet of Jesus Christ. Start by engaging with the Holy Spirit and sit at the feet of Jesus ready to receive all He has for you today. He is your comforter!

Devotional Sixty-Two

Revelation!

⁹Keep putting into practice all you learned and received from me—everything you heard from me and saw me doing. Then the God of peace will be with you.

(Philippians 4:9 NLT)

Dear Lord, please teach me the way to go. Lead me along still waters I pray and cause me to truly impact the world. Amen

Greetings to you my dear Brothers and Sisters in Christ Jesus. What joy it is to know God. I have realised that I don't truly know Him as I should. There's so much work to be done.

Imagine a child living life alone without being able to share deep truths and secrets with his/her father or mother. It is important to adopt the lifestyle of communing with your Heavenly Father and live a life of transparency.

On this path of righteousness, we are all working to know Him more. No one can truly say "I know God". The more you spend with Him, the more you get to know who He is. If you fall along the way, pick yourself up and continue the journey with God.

If at first you don't succeed, try again. Remember that Rome wasn't built in a day. Allow God refine and transform you completely by yielding daily to His word. Do not let the devil rob you anymore. It is time you take charge and move obediently as led by God.

You are more than able to do all you set out to do if you remain rooted and grounded in Christ Jesus. Remember you are the branch and Jesus Christ is the true vine. Without Him, you cease to exist.

Take all to God in prayer and He will reveal the truth about your life to you. Go to God in prayer!

Devotional Sixty-Three

Knowledge!

¹⁶It is senseless to pay to educate a fool, since he has no heart for learning. ¹⁹Anyone who loves to quarrel loves sin; anyone who trusts in high walls invites disaster.

(Proverbs 17:16, 19 NLT)

Greetings to you my beloved family in Christ Jesus. What do you have in your hands now? This message is bigger than you can imagine. Therefore, reflect on it asking the Holy Spirit to open your eyes to the truth in the message.

What has been given unto you to do? Yesterday, the Holy Spirit shed light on few areas of my life. He highlighted some of the talents God had given unto me. This revelation was an eye-opener as I didn't know I had work to do in the areas presented to me. Infact, I was so sure I knew what God required until today.

Therefore ask the Holy Spirit to show you that which has been given unto you to do. You can no longer gamble with your life. Remember that you only have one shot to get it right. Jesus is coming soon and my prayer is that we will all be ready when He returns.

I am far from where God needs me to be but determined to press on regardless to know Him more. David failed many times but returned to the feet of the Father. You cannot afford to live in denial. Cry out for insight and this will be given to you.

Philippians 3:12-16 MSG says, "Friends, don't get me wrong: by no means do I count myself an expert in all of this, but I've got my eye on the goal, where God is beckoning us onward—to Jesus. I'm off and running, and I'm not turning back. So, let's keep focused on that goal, those of us who want everything God has for us. If any of you have something else in mind, something less than total commitment, God will clear your blurred vision—you'll see it yet! Now that we're on the right track, let's stay on it".

Work out your own salvation with fear and trembling. Meditate on God's word today and remain connected to Him as best as you can. For knowledge applied right is power. It is no longer ok existing with no purpose; you must live right and do all that the Lord has given unto you to do before He calls you home.

Act Right!

Devotional Sixty-Four

What Do You Have in Your Hands?

¹⁶So we have stopped evaluating others from a human point of view. At one time we thought of Christ merely from a human point of view. How differently we know him now! ¹⁷This means that anyone who belongs to Christ has become a new person. The old life is gone; a new life has begun! ¹⁸And all of this is a gift from God, who brought us back to himself through Christ. And God has given us this task of reconciling people to him.

(2 Corinthians 5:16-18 NLT)

Greetings to you my beloved family in Christ Jesus. I write you with joy in my heart for I know that my redeemer lives. What about you?

The hour of growth has come but I'm afraid to say that many will miss it due to lack of knowledge. It is important to know and understand the seasons and times in order to be effective. Rise and enquire of the Lord today.

What do you have in your hands? What has God given you to do? What talents have you been given? Are you one living in denial or confusion? You see the talents in others but fail to see any in your life. Now is the time to open your eyes and see aright.

As I laid down on the sofa yesterday, the Holy Spirit dropped this into my heart. Your marriage, your children, your disciples and many more are the talents I have given you. He said I had failed to see the talents gifted unto me and that now is the time to work on multiplying all before the return of the Master.

You see the truth of the matter is you cannot be effective with anything you don't value. You must value the little God has given you in order for multiplication to come. You cannot go around desiring what others have without appreciating what He has given unto you. Therefore, I ask this honest question today: what comes easy to you? What are you very good at doing? What has been revealed unto you to do? Why not start with the little you know and do it well?

Now is the time of growth. You cannot remain a babe forever as Paul said in Corinthians. We must grow in Him. It is important to start feeding on meat and step out of the realm of drinking milk. Growth is essential for the next level. Even though the task might seem hard, remember that He wouldn't give you more than you can handle.

Work now with what you have and see the evidence of His power in your life. Yes, with the little, abundance will come if you learn to truly depend on Him. He bringeth harvest at the appointed time. All you need to do is plant and water the seeds with His Word ensuring it grows as the Lord intends. Manage the talents placed in your hands. Take charge now!

Devotional Sixty-Five

What Do You Allow into Your Heart?

¹¹Yes, you will be enriched in every way so that you can always be generous. And when we take your gifts to those who need them, they will thank God. ¹²So two good things will result from this ministry of giving—the needs of the believers in Jerusalem[f] will be met, and they will joyfully express their thanks to God.

(2 Corinthians 9:11-12 NLT)

Greetings to you my beloved Brothers and Sisters in Christ Jesus. Today's message is centred around the human heart. What do you allow to settle in your heart? What have you become accustomed to? What have you accepted as the norm in your heart?

I remember the challenges I faced as a child, I hated it when anyone cursed or called me words contrary to God's Word. I boldly annulled such words by rebuking it instantly. Many called me rebellious and naughty, but the truth of the matter is that I wasn't ready to accept the lies of the enemy as my truth.

What have you accepted as the norm? Many believe they are not good enough because of their many years of abuse. For how long will you be a slave to fear? The time has come to carefully weigh the words spoken to you and the words you allow settle in your heart. Decide now!

Who do you call friends and what words do they sow into your life? Do they curse you jokingly or call you names unknowingly? Now is the time to assess your associations. What do you spend time doing when you meet up with your friends? If you are one who sows gossip and rumours, now is the time to change your ways. Are you one who loves and encourages malice? Now is the time to turn from your wicked ways.

You cannot go around talking about everybody without receiving the same treatment from others. Whatever you sow, that you shall reap. You must set your mind free from the chains that hold you down.

Forgive and be forgiven.

Love and be loved.

Give and receive.

Now is the time to carefully weigh your actions. Are you living a life pleasing unto God or man? Go to God in prayer and ask for the grace and ability to see the true state of your heart. Trust me when I say you might not like what you see.

You cannot associate with lemons and remain sweet. The more you hang around lemons, the sour you become. This is the truth, and it is here to set you free.

Devotional Sixty-Six

Are You Firmly Rooted in His Word?

⁶Remember this—a farmer who plants only a few seeds will get a small crop. But the one who plants generously will get a generous crop. ⁷You must each decide in your heart how much to give. And don't give reluctantly or in response to pressure. "For God loves a person who gives cheerfully." ⁸And God will generously provide all you need. Then you will always have everything you need and plenty left over to share with others.

(2 Corinthians 9:6-8 NLT)

Greetings to you my blessed family in Christ Jesus. The time has come to do the needful. What is God's plan for you this season? Do you know His plan? Now is the time to engage with God to walk according to His perfect will.

This is the time to draw near to God. Are you firmly rooted in His Word? Now is the time to fix your altar. You cannot afford to be far from God this season. For the enemy is out to kill, steal and destroy. If you are for God, you must live aright following the examples laid down by Christ Jesus.

Embrace the Word.

Speak the Word.

Believe the Word now and live as instructed.

John 17:17-19 NLT says, "Make them holy by your truth; teach them your word, which is truth. Just as you sent me into the world, I am sending them into the world. And I give myself as a holy sacrifice for them so they can be made holy by your truth".

Now is the time to embrace the truth and be free from every slavery and limitation. You are what God says you are. It is important to know the Word and walk in it.

Come closer, let us return to the Lord now that He is near. The call is for those who want to go deeper. Do you want to experience God in a mighty way? If yes, press in today by studying His Word day and night. Meditate on His Word and live according to its instructions.

Get ready now! Store up treasures in Heaven and not on Earth. Know the truth and be free indeed!

Devotional Sixty-Seven

Amend Bridges

[11]Yes, you will be enriched in every way so that you can always be generous. And when we take your gifts to those who need them, they will thank God.

(2 Corinthians 9:11 NLT)

Greetings to you my beloved family in Christ. For the time has come to amend all bridges. Who have you offended or who has offended you? Now is the time to build by forgiving and forgetting all the wrongs done to you.

Go back and fix the past. Many are fond of moving away from the past without fixing bridges. In fact, many say and believe they can love others from a distance, but is that true? Is that what Christ instructed you to do? Did Jesus love from a distance? How long will you harbour unforgiveness in your heart? How long will you nurture that pain?

Yes, I know you were wronged, and it hurts bringing it back but isn't it better to fix it whilst you have life than wait for Jesus to appear and find you asleep? Jesus Christ is coming for a spotless and blameless church. Are you ready? Everything is visible to him so why not fix that which needs to be fixed now that you can. Delay no more, move now.

With the noise of death all around, isn't it a good time to fix all bridges? My family, I beseech you to please find it in your heart to forgive all who have wronged you now. Call and put to death every evil desire. Yes, they stabbed you and stole what was rightfully yours, why not forgive and hand them over to God. Allow God to fix them in His own time and way.

Vengeance is not the way of the godly, therefore continue to work out your own salvation with fear and trembling by asking the Holy Spirit to open your eyes to the wrongs you do. Take no offence instead drop the weights that hold you down. Forgive and be forgiven by God.

Devotional Sixty-Eight

And this Too Shall Come to Pass

¹⁰I want to know Christ and experience the mighty power that raised him from the dead. I want to suffer with him, sharing in his death, ¹¹so that one way or another I will experience the resurrection from the dead! ¹²I don't mean to say that I have already achieved these things or that I have already reached perfection. But I press on to possess that perfection for which Christ Jesus first possessed me. ¹⁴I press on to reach the end of the race and receive the heavenly prize for which God, through Christ Jesus, is calling us. ¹⁵Let all who are spiritually mature agree on these things. If you disagree on some point, I believe God will make it plain to you. ¹⁶But we must hold on to the progress we have already made.

(Philippians 3:10-12, 14-16 NLT)

Greetings to you my beloved family in Christ Jesus. That which you are trusting God for will surely come to pass if you can master the act of waiting on Him. How do you wait aright? By thanking Him for all that He has done in ages past, thanking Him for what He would do and expecting the manifestation of His love in your life.

How do you fix your eyes on Jesus? Many claim it is difficult especially when life is hard and unbearable. It is possible to fix your eyes on Jesus if you work with the Holy Spirit. You need to trust the Holy Spirit and allow Him to guide and lead you on the path of righteousness.

Come, let us return to the Lord.

Come, let us align with His will.

Come, let us please the Lord.

Now is the time to ask the Holy Spirit for help to move as directed. You cannot go about using your wisdom or understanding if you truly want victory. "Trust in the Lord with all your heart and lean not on your own understanding".

For How long will you toil that mountain? How long will you remain in that pit? Now is the time to truly abide under the shadow of the Almighty by relying on the leadership and assistance of the Holy Spirit. Ask for grace to abide and remain obedient to the Holy Spirit.

I was instructed to do nothing but heard otherwise days ago. I launched out in faith but kept asking whether it was God's will or mine. You see, the truth is that anyone can get it wrong therefore embrace the lifestyle of constant enquiry. Ask God at all times whether you are still aligned and connected to Him. Ask and keep asking then move as directed.

Finally, never assume you know the way instead ask until God provides clarity before you move. You cannot lead the Holy Spirit if you truly want victory. You must be led by the Holy Spirit to truly come out victorious. Therefore, repent and commit your ways to God. For many are wasting away by the seconds, no one knows tomorrow. Act now! Act fast!

God bless and keep you.

Devotional Sixty-Nine

God Is Doing Something New

¹⁷So I am not the one doing wrong; it is sin living in me that does it. ¹⁸And I know that nothing good lives in me, that is, in my sinful nature. I want to do what is right, but I can't. ¹⁹I want to do what is good, but I don't. I don't want to do what is wrong, but I do it anyway.

(Romans 7:17-19 NLT)

Greetings to you my beloved brothers and sisters in Christ Jesus. I was instructed to charge my phone as a matter of urgency. The reason isn't known to me yet, but I obeyed and charged it as directed. Do you listen to the Holy Spirit when He directs and instructs on the way to go?

Many pray to be led by the Spirit of God but are not ready to yield completely to Him. Who do you follow, God or Man? Many follow the enemy without their knowledge. Now is the time to know the truth. David prayed in Psalm 139:23-24 saying, "Search me God and know my heart; test me and know my anxious thoughts. See if there is any offensive way in me and lead me in the way everlasting".

Trust and obey the one who says, "I am doing something new in your life".

I have always had a problem with following people blindly. In fact, if God doesn't direct, I will remain still until instructed otherwise. I have learned to follow God completely to receive in abundance. When He says begin to dream again, it is important to commence the act of dreaming.

I have allowed many things slip past me this year but this time I am willing and determined to follow God all the way. I submit to His lordship and will go wherever He sends me. For I have come to know that I am nothing without Him. What about you? Are you willing to follow Him completely?

Finally, believe His Word spoken over your life and start dreaming again. All things are working together for your good. It is important to remain submissive to the leadership of the Holy Spirit to experience all that the Lord has in store for you this year.

He is able to turn your life around for good. God Almighty "Jehovah" is His name, and He is ready to move on your behalf. Rely solely on Him by trusting Him completely.

Devotional Seventy

Go Back to the Basics

¹⁰And now he has made all of this plain to us by the appearing of Christ Jesus, our Savior. He broke the power of death and illuminated the way to life and immortality through the Good News. ¹¹And God chose me to be a preacher, an apostle, and a teacher of this Good News. ¹²That is why I am suffering here in prison. But I am not ashamed of it, for I know the one in whom I trust, and I am sure that he is able to guard what I have entrusted to him until the day of his return.

(2 Timothy 1:10-12 NLT)

Greetings to you my beloved family in Christ Jesus. Have you asked God why you are here on earth and what He has planned for you? Now is the time to ask in order to know His will for your life.

Many find themselves running other people's race because they haven't mastered the act of truly waiting on God for insight before moving. Are you just a follower? Who do you follow? Have you ever asked God? If you follow a blind shepherd or leader, you will eventually fall into destruction.

How can you follow one you don't really know? Many claim to be saved but know nothing about the one who saved them. Time truly waits for no one. I have watched the year fly past before my eyes. Isn't it best to know God's plan before heading into the later months of this year? Ask yourself and give yourself an honest answer. Is this truly the best of you? Do you have more to give? What is holding you back?

Many hide under the lack of money but if you were presented a million pounds today, what would you use it for? Have you done your research whilst you wait? Do you have any dreams? Have you given up on the future because of your situation today? Now is the time to retrace your tracks. Find out how and why you are where you are today.

Now is the time to truly know. Arise and begin to dream again. Ask for God's will and walk in alignment with His will. Join me in dreaming today, get a clean new slate and start drawing the future you desire to see. The key is in your hands. You must first see it before you can receive it.

Finally, ask God for insight about who you follow and move accordingly.

Devotional Seventy-One

Be Inspired

¹¹Now these are the gifts Christ gave to the church: the apostles, the prophets, the evangelists, and the pastors and teachers. ¹²Their responsibility is to equip God's people to do his work and build up the church, the body of Christ. ¹³This will continue until we all come to such unity in our faith and knowledge of God's Son that we will be mature in the Lord, measuring up to the full and complete standard of Christ.

(Ephesians 4:11-13 NLT)

Greetings to you my beloved family in Christ. For a new day has come, rejoice I say rejoice. How can you rejoice when all around you seems discouraging? This is possible if you abide under the shadow of the Almighty. Knowledge of your position in God keeps you joyful and thankful. You are not just anyone but one with great substance and a great God who abides with you.

Are you weary and unable to dream? Today's message is here to inspire and encourage you. Yes, I know and understand that life could be challenging. The truth of the matter is some will have more whilst others will have less. This is just life but understanding how to survive at both spectrums is key to survival as a Child of God. You have the ability to dream and live as desired because you serve a mighty God.

For Scripture says that in the beginning, the earth was void and without form until God declared light into existence. Darkness was always present, but the appearance of light brought about change and newness. Light comes when you believe God's Word. Today is an opportunity to bring forth light into every dark patch or uncertainty. Speak it forth and walk by faith.

For the righteous know their God and do great exploits. Knowledge of God Almighty is key to survival in the storm. For the storm is present to kill and destabilise the body of Christ. Those who know their God will do great exploits. Do you know your God? Or are you one who is taking chances by living life as you please hoping that all good things will fall at your feet. Think again!

There's more to life than gold and silver. Now is the time to know in order to dream that which the Lord originally planned for you. God bless you as you spend time with your Father to truly know Him. Draw near and He will draw near to you.

Devotional Seventy-Two

Do the Needful and Rest

¹⁹And this same God who takes care of me will supply all your needs from his glorious riches, which have been given to us in Christ Jesus.

(Philippians 4:19 NLT)

Greetings to you my family in Christ Jesus. For the joy of the Lord is your strength. Rest in Him today!

What is that thing you have put on hold or avoided for so long? Why not face it today and do the needful? Rely not on your strength to do or complete that which you desire to do but trust in the Lord as best as you can and move as led. For He is able and ever ready to help you.

Yes, it is impossible to please God without faith. Why then have you stopped believing in yourself? It is time you dig into the unlimited resources available on the inside of you. You are more than a conqueror, but you must believe that you are no longer alone. You have a God who will never leave you nor forsake you. You are surrounded by all the goodness and blessings you can ever imagine. Do you see it?

Waste no more time looking to man for help. Did that friend promise to help you but fail to keep his/her promise? Worry not. Dust your feet and press forward in faith. Believe in the one true God who is readily available to help you out of the ditch. He says, "come unto me ye who are heavily burdened, and I will give you rest".

After doing all, rest in Him. Wait for the appointed time for it will surely come. That which you are trusting God for this season will fall on your laps sooner than you can imagine. Oh, my brothers and sisters in Christ, it pays to trust in God Almighty all the way. Leave no stone unturned. Run the race set before you with all that you have been given. You have the power to do all. Just believe and move today.

Devotional Seventy-Three

Make an Effort

¹⁷This is my command: Love each other.

(John 15:17 NLT)

Greetings to you my beloved family in Christ Jesus. Who do you call a friend? You cannot love what you don't value. Today's message is centred around love. Love is the greatest command of all.

How can you say you love like Christ but make no time to call or visit your loved ones? Now is the time to act out the love you claim to have. Now is the time to show someone you love and care about them. Now is the time to be your brother's keeper.

Quit talking, start acting!

Today's message is straight to the point. Love cannot just remain in your heart. If you truly love, then all must see and know that indeed you love. Many are hurting today and going through emotional distress, pain and frustration; are you paying attention to the needs of those you call friends?

Let us endeavour to love.

Be like Christ Jesus who made out time to be with the poor and needy. He truly loved whilst on earth and all saw that He was good.

Why don't you start by paying someone a visit today? Let us spread love as best as we can. Help those in need and let us make the world a better place together.

I need you and you need me to survive. Act now!

Devotional Seventy-Four

Your Gifts

¹⁴When I think of all this, I fall to my knees and pray to the Father, ¹⁶I pray that from his glorious, unlimited resources he will empower you with inner strength through his Spirit. ¹⁷Then Christ will make his home in your hearts as you trust in him. Your roots will grow down into God's love and keep you strong.

(Ephesians 3:14, 16-17 NLT)

Greetings to you my beloved family in Christ Jesus. What are your gifts? Come let us reason together. For God has deposited so much on the inside of you, do you see it? You cannot continue looking down on your gifts. For you have more than you think on the inside of you. Yes, you do!

I was laying down feeling sorry for myself and unable to stay awake until I stumbled on a programme highlighting the gifts of a woman. You see, the truth is that one of the gifts given to me by God is the ability to write. Writing comes naturally to me when inspired by the Holy Spirit hence why you have an opportunity to read from me daily. So, I am grateful to Him for this gift. It might be one in a million but this one is of great value and importance to me therefore I will cherish it as best as I can and so should you.

What are you good at? What comes easy or natural to you? Now is the time to look inwardly in order to see what God has given unto you freely. Once you discover it, ask for the grace to develop it. Work at it and begin to move as led by the Holy Spirit.

This journey of salvation is a practical lifestyle. You cannot speak the Word without truly living it. Now is the time to bring your gift to life. Call it forth and multiply that which you have been given. Get busy!

Finally, if you believe you have greatness on the inside of you, now is the time to live it out. Please look inside and bring to life all that you have in abundance. You truly are worth more than you can ever imagine or think. Embrace your gifts and watch them multiply. For the Master is waiting to see what you have done with the talents given unto you. Make it matter. Get busy!

God bless you as you do so. You are truly loved and remember that He will make provision for the entirety of the journey. He is able!

Devotional Seventy-Five

Clear Out the Weed

⁹So let's not get tired of doing what is good. At just the right time we will reap a harvest of blessing if we don't give up. ¹⁶May God's peace and mercy be upon all who live by this principle; they are the new people of God.

(Galatians 6:9, 16 NLT)

You see, the trouble with sleeping is that whilst the farmer sleeps, the weed spoils the vine. How long do you intend on sleeping? Sleeping in this context could be likened to discouragement, fear, slumber, being lukewarm etc. The truth of the matter is that the Body of Christ cannot afford to be disconnected from the vine. The longer you stay disconnected equates to the drier you become and dry branches eventually lose their holding force and fall off the vine.

Jesus is the true vine, and we are the branches. This message is to call you and I back home. You see praying with a doubtful mind is as good as not praying. You cannot say you love the Lord with all your heart and mind but live in fear of the unknown. O brethren, come and let us reason today. Is it possible for a child raised in a loving home to forget his/her father? Of course not. Yes, you were once hot but how long will you allow or permit this separation from God. Isn't it time you draw near to the source of life? Come up hither!

You wonder how you are surviving. Isn't it the light that still dwells on the inside of you that keeps you moving? Waste no more time for the oil is running out. It is time to come to the throne room of grace for a refreshing. It is a choice! Are you ready for the refreshing? Are you ready to change posture and allow the Holy Spirit to take over the driving seat of your life?

Are you still doubtful about tomorrow? If He made yesterday possible and permitted you to witness today, is He not able to perfect tomorrow? Did you help Him in perfecting yesterday? If not, why not entrust tomorrow into His hands. God is able to do exceedingly, abundantly above all that you could ever ask or think. Quit looking down on God by welcoming doubt, fear and unbelief.

Arise and begin to uproot the weed that has disfigured and spoilt the vine. Rise and run away from condemnation. The truth of the matter is that God's plan is certain for those who believe. Believe!

Devotional Seventy-Six

Rainbow

¹⁴So then, since we have a great High Priest who has entered heaven, Jesus the Son of God, let us hold firmly to what we believe. ¹⁵This High Priest of ours understands our weaknesses, for he faced all of the same testings we do, yet he did not sin. ¹⁶So let us come boldly to the throne of our gracious God. There we will receive his mercy, and we will find grace to help us when we need it most.

(Hebrews 4:14-16 NLT)

Greetings to you my family in Christ. Today has been a real eye-opener for me. I woke up feeling discouraged and unable to smile. I kept looking for a reason to smile but couldn't find any. I looked but felt worse than ever until a rainbow appeared. A gigantic rainbow appeared before me and I remembered the promises of God over my life. God knew exactly what I needed to brighten my mood. What joy it is to know that I have a God who is alive and present.

Where are you today? Are you discouraged and overwhelmed? I am here to encourage you this day. The Holy Spirit is available to help you out of that pit. Just call on Him and He will help you today. Weeping may endure for a night but joy cometh in the morning. Rest in His Word. God is still in the business of doing mighty miracles. Just believe!

Scripture says, "Rejoice in the Lord always". How possible is it to rejoice when all around you seems discouraging and overwhelming? By holding God to His Word. Count all your blessings and name them one by one. God is so faithful to fail His own. He wouldn't bring you this far to leave you. He is not a mean God but a good Father who is with you all the time. Trust that He is working things out for your good and wait patiently not by your power but by total reliance on the Holy Spirit that dwells on the inside of you. Do you believe?

Keep trusting.

Keep waiting.

Keep believing.

Keep hoping for the best. For all you desire will be granted as long as you continue trusting and believing in Him. Stand and keep standing on His Word until all that you desire manifests before your eyes. He is still in the business of turning lives around.

He is too faithful to fail you.

He is too faithful to disappoint you.

You are here to serve Him therefore cling unto Him and find strength in Him. Remain blessed.

Devotional Seventy-Seven

Fight for Your Life

¹⁵I have seen everything in this meaningless life, including the death of good young people and the long life of wicked people. ¹⁶So don't be too good or too wise! Why destroy yourself? ¹⁷On the other hand, don't be too wicked either. Don't be a fool! Why die before your time? ¹⁸Pay attention to these instructions, for anyone who fears God will avoid both extremes. ¹⁹One wise person is stronger than ten leading citizens of a town!

(Ecclesiastes 7:15-19 NLT)

Greetings to you my beloved family in Christ Jesus. Awake from your sleep my brothers and sisters and begin to see the goodness of God around you. Has He said and not done it? Ask yourself this question today. Think back and thank Him for all He has done for you. He is truly a good Father.

You may ask why I am confident and positive about this God. For He has proven Himself over and over again in my life. All that I am and will ever be is down to His goodness and mercy over my life. This is why I can't come here with a negative mentality or discouraged heart. For He has been too good to me and still remains good. What about you? Has the Lord been good to you?

Taste and see that the Lord is good. For His goodness and mercy endureth forever. What do you want to see happen in your life? Start dreaming, start building that desire and never feel bad for dreaming big. You hold the power to dream, utilise it as best as you can and wait for the appointed time of manifestation.

Go, gather all you have and present it to the Most High God. If He could do it for one, He can do it for you too. God is still in the business of surprising and blessing His own. Get ready for the abundance of goodness in all you set out to you. He handles the affairs of men if presented to Him. God will not force Himself on you instead He invites you to come closer in order to see all that is accessible for His own.

Fight for your future.

Fight for your children.

Fight to keep yourself relevant and valuable this season.

Make a difference by praying for a life or two this day. Choose not to focus on yourself but reach out to a life in need. For there's more to this than meets the eye therefore run closer and find rest in Him.

Many would ask how to fight. You fight by staying connected to God, believing His Word and meditating on it, staying connected to God minded people, consciously seek His face for clarity and moving as led. His Word says that we should put on the whole armour of God at all times in order to remain standing at the end of the storm. For the enemy is out to steal, kill and destroy.

Devotional Seventy-Eight

Revert Back

¹⁸Don't be drunk with wine, because that will ruin your life. Instead, be filled with the Holy Spirit, ¹⁹singing psalms and hymns and spiritual songs among yourselves, and making music to the Lord in your hearts.

(Ephesians 5:18-19 NLT)

Greetings to you my family in Christ Jesus. Today's message is to encourage you to dig deeper. Take out time to truly know your position and spiritual health. Are you healthy or unhealthy? Are you aching or strong with the ability to help others? What is your status today?

As I laid back on my sofa, I realised I had been detached from my source. For Jesus is the way, the truth and the life. I had allowed circumstances and the busyness of life to detach me from the one true God. Jehovah is so rich in mercy and readily available to bring all back to the place purposed and destined.

Where are you today? Now is the time to revert back in order to fix the gaps. For many have sinned and fallen short of the glory of God. Are you one who has allowed sin to detach you from the vine? For Jesus is the true vine and we are the branches. Without the vine, the branches cease to exist.

Don't be misled by the gifts you exhibit. Yes, you have the gift of prophecy, but are you where God needs you to be now? The call is for those who have ears and are willing to turn from their ways of old. Let us run the race set before us looking not at our present needs or circumstances but focusing on Jesus Christ who has been made as an authority over us.

I have come to understand that we truly need to associate with the right company to remain active in the midst of the storm. Yes, Jesus is the way but why have you detached yourself from those he gave unto you as destiny helpers? Rome wasn't built in a day. It took time and effort to build and so do relationships. Spend quality time with the true vine and become more like Him. Now is the time!

You need me and I need you to survive. Retract!

Devotional Seventy-Nine

What Did God Say?

^{13}For I can do everything through Christ, who gives me strength. ^{19}And this same God who takes care of me will supply all your needs from his glorious riches, which have been given to us in Christ Jesus.

(Philippians 4:13, 19 NLT)

Greeting to you my beloved family in Christ Jesus. Ever wondered what life would be like without your loved ones? Now is the time to appreciate God for everything, even the little given unto you.

Do you question whether God truly loves you because of your challenges? In fact, many believe challenges and tests are solely from the enemy, lies! That challenge you are going through has a foundation. Now is the time to ask God for clarity and move according to His instructions of the Spirit.

What has God said about that matter? Could fixing a wrong truly fix your pressing challenges? A few days ago, the Holy Spirit shared the real reason behind a pressing need. He said the delay was due to my disobedience and unwillingness to move as directed. Could this be you as well?

What is truly stopping you from moving forward? Fear, pride, unbelief, doubt? Ask yourself and then ask the Holy Spirit for grace to step out of the old into the new. Step forward and refrain from looking back.

Finally, how have you spent the last 6 months? Can you honestly say you have maximised it as best as you can? I unashamedly say that I haven't used the last 6 months well but pray for the grace to use the next 3 months wisely. I am determined to move as led and ask for insight before setting out.

Therefore, let us determine in our hearts to follow the leadership of God Almighty. Let us enquire until we truly know the way to go. Let us stop using our own understanding but rely solely on the Holy Spirit. If you are yet to hear from God, keep knocking on the door until the door is open unto you. It surely will as long as you refrain from using your own reasoning and giving up.

If at first, you don't succeed, try again!

Devotional Eighty

Take Action

14So then, since we have a great High Priest who has entered heaven, Jesus the Son of God, let us hold firmly to what we believe. 15This High Priest of ours understands our weaknesses, for he faced all of the same testings we do, yet he did not sin.

(Hebrews 4:14-15 NLT)

Greetings to you my beloved family in Christ Jesus. This is the day the Lord has made meaning He chose to create a day for you to witness. Rejoice I say Rejoice!

Rejoice when you have nothing in your bank account.

Rejoice when your children are playing up and acting contrary to the Word of the Lord.

Rejoice when your current situation is no way close to your desired situation. Just rejoice!

Rejoice I say Rejoice.

Ask God for strength to remain joyful even in the midst of the storm.

You see, the act of rejoicing in the midst of chaos is a choice. You are not rejoicing because you like your current situation but rejoicing because you trust that God has things under control and His plans are working together for your good. Trust is key!

Gather your strength this day and decide to smile. Gather your strength as you read this message today. Take out time to encourage someone today. Where there's life, there's hope.

Is anything too hard for God? Ask yourself today and rely solely on His promises.

Devotional Eighty-One

What Do You Do When the Going Gets Tough?

¹³So please don't lose heart because of my trials here. I am suffering for you, so you should feel honoured. ¹⁶I pray that from his glorious, unlimited resources he will empower you with inner strength through his Spirit. ¹⁷Then Christ will make his home in your hearts as you trust in him. Your roots will grow down into God's love and keep you strong.

(Ephesians 3:13, 16-17 NLT)

Greetings to you my Brothers and Sisters in Christ Jesus. What do you do when all comes crashing down? Do you give up on God and run to the next big thing? Reflect on this today and honestly answer the question in your heart. The truth is that we are created for His pleasure meaning that He is not serving us, but we are created to serve Him.

If we are truly created to please Him, shouldn't we ask what pleases Him and how He would like us to conduct ourselves in the land of the living? Instead, we go around acting like God owes us a favour and works for us. God owes us nothing, family. He chose to love us unconditionally regardless of our rights or wrongs. He chose to create us in His image. He chose to let us experience this year with the problems and chaos around. It is His choice, and He understands what we are all going through this very moment.

Today's message is not to discourage but encourage you to rise and live for Him and not yourself. God truly owes you nothing. How we live in the storm determines the level of our love and trust in Him. Do you truly love this God? Do you truly know this God? Are you truly prepared to stand with Him even when your world comes crashing down?

I struggled to dream a few weeks back. In fact, I realised that my faith wasn't as big as a mustard seed. I realised that all I claimed to be was just a facade and built on lies. I realised that I served God because of His goodness and kindness towards me. What a journey!

As I gazed at the sky feeling sorry for myself, He said, "Maria, now is the time to dream again". This was one of the hardest assignments ever. I couldn't dream because I couldn't see beyond my current struggles and pain until I remembered that it is not by my power or might that I am able to function on this road of salvation.

I sat down with my book wide open, Lord please help me dream again. I prayed and suddenly, I started dreaming. What joy it is to see again. What joy it is to hope in the Great Unseen God. He is Jehovah "God Almighty".

Dream again!

Devotional Eighty-Two

Sit Down and Get on With It

¹¹A hard worker has plenty of food, but a person who chases fantasies has no sense.

(Proverbs 12:11 NLT)

What is that task you have put on hold for so long?

What is that matter you have overlooked for so long?

Now is the time to sit and act.

One would question why there's a need to sit. To sit in this context means to trust that God has things under control. Once you believe and know this, the act of sitting would become easy. Sit and act!

Ask for guidance and launch out into the deep.

Quit settling for small things. It's either you know who you are or not. Who are you?

As for me, I am a daughter of the Most High God meaning that the best is mine. In my Father's kingdom, there's no limitation and struggle. Others might settle for less, but I can't and wouldn't. For my Father is Master of the whole universe. If you see it, you can receive it. Now is the time to act!

For so long you have watched others accelerate leaving you behind and you wonder why God hasn't done anything for you.

Yes, you have prayed, fasted and even sowed a seed or two towards that promotion but nothing has happened. Sit and let us reason together. Of what use is it to pray and not have the ability to act.

When you pray, you must spend time waiting to hear from your Father. Prayer is a two-way stream not one-way. Therefore, you must act as He instructs you. When He says launch out, you must move accordingly. Do exactly what your Father says when He speaks.

I tried calling my Spiritual mentor few times this week and was unable to reach him. This almost broke me as I had an important matter to discuss with him then this thought hit me, what if God was silent to me and unavailable for me, how would I live or exist? It is important to seek God whilst He is near. Quit making excuses or procrastinating! Now is the time to act. Start studying that bible or book you had hoped to read for so long.

Waste no more time thinking about your imperfections instead believe you can do all you set out to do then act. So, you have longed for that managerial position, what are the steps required to get there? Now is the time to know and act accordingly. Take that step now!

Devotional Eighty-Three

Is Your Oil Running Out?

²⁴Here is another story Jesus told: "The Kingdom of Heaven is like a farmer who planted good seed in his field. ²⁵But that night as the workers slept, his enemy came and planted weeds among the wheat, then slipped away. ²⁶When the crop began to grow and produce grain; the weeds also grew. ²⁷"The farmer's workers went to him and said, 'Sir, the field where you planted that good seed is full of weeds! Where did they come from?' ³⁷Jesus replied, "The Son of Man[d] is the farmer who plants the good seed. ³⁸The field is the world, and the good seed represents the people of the Kingdom. The weeds are the people who belong to the evil one. ³⁹The enemy who planted the weeds among the wheat is the devil. The harvest is the end of the world, and the harvesters are the angels.

(Matthew 13:24-27, 37-39 NLT)

Ever imagined what the 5 virgins were thinking when they slept without oils in their lamps? I believe they slept because they had waited for the groom for long and grown tired of waiting believing He would come later and not anytime soon.

Isn't this exactly how most of us are today? We know that we have been given talents but are yet to spend quality time with God in order to understand our detailed tasks. How long would you and I procrastinate? Don't you know Christ Jesus can come anytime? Are you ready? Have you multiplied your talents? Where are you today?

Are you sitting there feeling sorry for yourself? I spent most of yesterday complaining and moaning. If Jesus had appeared, where exactly would I be? He said, be anxious for nothing. Why then are you overwhelmed and unable to dream? Why are you so downcast and unprepared? Don't you know that this is the allotted time to seek God in order to understand your purpose here on earth? Time is running fast, get on with what God has given you to do.

You can no longer waste your precious time. No one knows how long they have on earth. Let us make today count. Start acting and stop waiting for a good weather condition to sow. Now is the time to draw near to God than ever before. Quit complaining instead reach out to the Holy Spirit and move as led. Be wise as a serpent. Draw closer to the Holy Spirit and allow Him to fill you afresh. Work out your own salvation with fear and trembling knowing that the King of Kings will come unannounced and expects you and I to be prepared.

Though it's not physically easy to put down the worries, I encourage you this day to entrust all into God's Hands. Keep asking for help and receive it when offered. The Holy Spirit is alive and willingly ready to bless whoever needs help. He will not force you to conform therefore you must desire to want Him more than the finer things of this world.

Finally, ensure your conduct, decisions and actions here on earth mirrors that of Jesus Christ. Go now, fill your lamps and remain expectant.

Devotional Eighty-Four

Go Tell It on the Mountain

¹¹I have observed something else under the sun. The fastest runner doesn't always win the race, and the strongest warrior doesn't always win the battle. The wise sometimes go hungry, and the skilful are not necessarily wealthy. And those who are educated don't always lead successful lives. It is all decided by chance, by being in the right place at the right time. ¹²People can never predict when hard times might come. Like fish in a net or birds in a trap, people are caught by sudden tragedy.

(Ecclesiastes 9:11-12 NLT)

Love is a command.

Do you really love like Christ Jesus or are you one who loves only when it's convenient?

Now is the time to speak and show love everywhere you go. Go out and spread love.

A few weeks back, I met a guy named Graham on my morning walk. He looked lost and disconnected from life. I walked past him initially until the Holy Spirit instructed me to go back and deliver a message to him. I approached him and spoke as led telling him how loved he was by His Father in heaven. As I walked down that same path today, I saw him again but this time, he recognised me and approached me with a big smile. What joy it was to see him smile and remember me.

Your smile might be what someone needs to realign themselves back to reality. Give as much as you can even when you have very little to give. Decide to make a difference today by reaching out to a life. Try even when you find it hard to move.

Go tell it on the mountain. Tell all you see and know that God loves and cares about them. They might not believe it but trust that the Holy Spirit will complete the work you have started in them. Do your part and leave the rest. Impact the world you live in today and truly make a difference.

God bless and keep you.

Devotional Eighty-Five

Take Baby Steps

17Better to hear the quiet words of a wise person than the shouts of a foolish king. 18Better to have wisdom than weapons of war, but one sinner can destroy much that is good.

(Ecclesiastes 9:17-18 NLT)

Greetings to you my blessed family in Christ Jesus. Ever beaten yourself up for wasting precious time and find yourself repeating the same cycle time and time again? Well, this too will end in Jesus mighty name amen.

I laid on my bed yesterday asking the Holy Spirit for strength. I asked for help to achieve and conquer but felt so weak to do anything. Ever felt like this? Rest! Today is the day that the Lord has made, and you will succeed in all you set out to do if you yield to the instructions given by the Holy Spirit.

Start your day by aligning yourself with the Holy Spirit. Consciously put on the whole armour of God then set out knowing that greater is He that is in you than He that is in the world. Write out the tasks you plan to do today and prayerfully take baby steps to achieve them one by one.

Worry not about yesterday instead try and keep trying to do better today. For yesterday has gone and today is here. Start your day with a positive mindset. Allow the Holy Spirit to lead you and determine in your heart to obey accordingly.

Do you have desires? What are the plans you have given up on? Pick them up again and start ticking them off one by one. You have the power to do all you set out to do if you believe you can. Press on like never before. If at first, you don't succeed, try again. Now is not the time to give up on your future.

Hope must rise.

Faith must rise.

In Jesus mighty name I pray Amen

Devotional Eighty-Six

Cleanliness

¹¹So if the old way, which has been replaced, was glorious, how much more glorious is the new, which remains forever! ¹²Since this new way gives us such confidence; we can be very bold.

(2 Corinthians 3:11-12 NLT)

Create in me a clean heart O Lord and renew a right spirit within me. This is the prayer of the day. Dear Lord, I acknowledge that I might have allowed sin into my heart such as unforgiveness, hate, anger, bitterness etc. Cleanse out everything that brings no pleasure to you today in Jesus mighty name. Amen.

Greetings to you my Brothers and Sisters in Christ Jesus. What is the state of your heart today? Let's do a quick check.

What has been your story till date? Have you been battered, abused, wrongly accused or harmed? I ask you this day to forgive all who have wronged you. The problem with hurt is that if it isn't addressed it could truly poison and harm the recipient. Yes, they have wronged you but why allow the wrong to destroy you? Forgive and be forgiven.

Now is the time to fix all that needs fixing in order for God to bring complete healing. Get your house in order and ensure it is as clean as possible. Bring out the broom and sweep away the trash. Quit hiding dirt under the bed, the chairs etc. Now is the time to bring it all out in the open in order to be completely healed.

Many are hiding memories that hurt and find it hard to share with others. Ask the Holy Spirit for help today and speak out. There is truly power in speaking out. I personally believe it is the beginning of one's healing. If you can talk about it then your healing process is closer to completion.

Let's get speaking. Many would ask "who can I trust? Who do I speak to?" Ask the Holy Spirit and He will direct you. Speak out and get that pain off your chest. Be healed and free from every pain today. For that pain is a bondage that keeps you tied down in the pit of darkness.

If you claim to be light why then do you give the enemy power by living like one in darkness? Decide what path you want to be and receive complete healing today. The day is here to address all matters that has crippled you.

Open up and begin to heal!

Keep no more painful secrets instead release yourself to the goodness of God's plan and desire for you. He cares and knows your name.

Devotional Eighty-Seven

Strap Up and Get Ready for the Ride

¹¹So let us do our best to enter that rest. But if we disobey God, as the people of Israel did, we will fall.

(Hebrews 4:11 NLT)

Ever jumped on a ride without strapping your belt? Impossible! In fact, some would call it a suicide plot if ever attempted or even imagined.

The Lord is saying to you and I today. Fasten your seatbelt and get ready for the adventure to come. For there's a plan mapped out for those who are ready for the Spiritual adventure. Allow God to take you on this ride. He has a plan for you and I. What great joy it is to be called sons and daughters of the Lord Most High.

How can you serve the Lord Most High and feel discouraged? For all that you will ever need is available in Him. All you need for the journey ahead has already been given to you. Get ready! The King of Kings is in charge and knows exactly what is reserved for you at each junction.

In fact, the Lord says that there are gifts wrapped for all at every junction. The longer you stay onboard equates to the number of gifts and blessings you receive. It is all yours but staying onboard requires complete trust and hope in God

Almighty. You must believe that He knows exactly what He is doing.

Sow with a view to righteousness [that righteousness, like a seed, may germinate]; Reap in accordance with mercy and lovingkindness. Break up your uncultivated ground, for it is time to seek and search diligently for the Lord [and to long for His blessing] Until He comes to rain righteousness and His gift of salvation on you. Hosea 10:12 AMP

Get busy doing what is required. Find God and stay with Him for the entire journey. Allow the Holy Spirit to strap you in. Sit and rest at His feet. Sow faithfulness and receive divine blessings and increase. Now is the time to know!

Are you still out there looking for someone like you? Worry no more for you were made in the image and likeness of God Most High. You are perfect just the way you are. Quit allowing the lies spoken to you to distract you from continuing the journey ahead. Love yourself and know who you are in Him.

Trust and obey!

Devotional Eighty-Eight

Decisions

¹⁵So be careful how you live. Don't live like fools, but like those who are wise. ¹⁶Make the most of every opportunity in these evil days. ¹⁷Don't act thoughtlessly, but understand what the Lord wants you to do.

(Ephesians 5:15-17 NLT)

Ever decided to make a change for the benefit of your future or children? There comes a time when one must decide what path to take and move as led. Now is the time!

I made a decision today which would eventually accelerate me to the next level. I decided to stop giving excuses and start making changes. Many Christians are fond of speaking the Word but not acting. We cannot afford to be hearers only therefore pick up your pen and begin to write. We ask God to move but do nothing. Really! How long would we live this way?

What do you need the most in life? Doesn't it baffle you that Solomon when asked this question, replied saying "Wisdom"? He understood that Wisdom was more profitable than silver and gold.

Solomon was truly one marked out for greatness. He was wise and he's one to observe if you're truly in search of wisdom. Aren't you tired of just existing? Rise up today and let God shine His light into your heart.

"How much better to get wisdom than gold, and good judgment than silver! The wise are known for their understanding, and pleasant words are persuasive. From a wise mind comes wise speech; the words of the wise are persuasive." Proverbs 16:16, 21, 23 NLT

Finally, decide to make a difference. Cease from just existing and start changing your world. Now is the time to rise from the place of dormancy to a place of action. Run the race set before you knowing that you did your very best with all you were given on earth.

Choose your friends wisely! Iron sharpeneth Iron. Have a blessed day.

Devotional Eighty-Nine

Follow Him

17Dear brothers and sisters, pattern your lives after mine, and learn from those who follow our example. 18For I have told you often before, and I say it again with tears in my eyes, that there are many whose conduct shows they are really enemies of the cross of Christ. 19They are headed for destruction. Their god is their appetite, they brag about shameful things, and they think only about this life here on earth.

(Philippians 3:17-19 NLT)

Greetings to you my family in Christ Jesus. How is life treating you? I have had a lot on my plate lately and struggling to balance things up. Are you going through a similar phase? Please take a deep breath and allow the Holy Spirit to direct you.

Life can be so overwhelming at times and it truly takes divine intervention and assistance to find one's bearing. I have come to realise that the only way one can truly excel in life is by following every instruction provided by the Holy Spirit. "Taste and see that the Lord is good".

To taste and see means you must decide to let go of your own thoughts and trust the process completely in order to see. God is saying "Do you love me enough to let go of your own ways and follow mine?". However stupid as it might sound, the key to unlimited breakthrough and success is obedience. You must decide to obey God completely.

I recently joined an organisation which has been an eye-opener for me but one thing I got from the training is that in order to succeed, you must be coachable. This is the same with the Kingdom of God. To pass the assignment given by God, you must be coachable. Jesus said, "Come and I will make you fishers of men". Obedience is required to come. God is calling you and I today "Come closer to know my plans for your life". Draw near that I draw near unto you. You must be determined to follow every example laid down by Jesus Christ adding nothing to it. This is the secret to pleasing the Father.

The Father is not looking for people who are too proud or struggle to follow orders. In fact, I was so quick to move when I joined the business, that I recorded a video following my own understanding. This was wrong because I didn't follow the manual. The video was my own creation based on my understanding which could lead others astray. For me to truly excel, I must let go of the old and welcome the new.

The summary of the message is this - complete obedience is required to pass the test. Pay close attention!

Devotional Ninety

He Said So!

¹¹Furthermore, because we are united with Christ, we have received an inheritance from God, for he chose us in advance, and he makes everything work out according to his plan.

(Ephesians 1:11 NLT)

Greetings to you my beloved family in Christ Jesus.

Do you have the patience required to finish the race? Do you ever think about the journey of the Israelites from Egypt to the promised land? One would say God was unfair to them, but the truth is that the promised land was already gifted unto them, all they had to do was believe and have faith that they would get there.

Despite the wonders performed on the way to the promised land, they doubted and murmured in their hearts. They questioned whether they had made the right decision in leaving Egypt. This is the same mistake most of us make when waiting on God. We give up easily and quit believing. This must change and change starts now.

What has God promised you? It is important to believe that it is already done and await the manifestation. Whilst waiting, ask the Holy Spirit for strength to endure the hardship and trials along the way. Delay is not denial and remember that whilst you wait, you must remain joyful and thankful knowing that all He said will be.

Faith is important on this journey. You cannot confess the Word without believing that it will be so. God needs you and I to exercise our faith by believing in Him than ever before. Come boldly into the throne room of grace today and receive favour. God is still in the business of doing wonders. Just believe!

What is that prayer request you are still trusting God to answer? Believe He has done it and keep knocking until the door is open unto you. Confess what you want to see and wait patiently. For it will surely come to pass. This is sure.

Devotional Ninety-One

Decisions (2)

²²Then Jesus said to the disciples, "Have faith in God. ²³I tell you the truth, you can say to this mountain, 'May you be lifted up and thrown into the sea,' and it will happen. But you must really believe it will happen and have no doubt in your heart. ²⁴I tell you, you can pray for anything, and if you believe that you've received it, it will be yours.

(Mark 11:22-24 NLT)

Knowledge is power if applied right. How do you apply knowledge without wisdom? The truth is that they work hand in hand. Wisdom and knowledge to act is key on the path of perfection and increase. Many are called but few are chosen.

We need to get to a point where we no longer feel comfortable with our current position or situation. We must desire greatness and act accordingly in order to be great. How long have you prayed for riches but find yourself begging for bread? Action is key! Wise counsel is key!

Gather and bring your best before the Lord today. What do you have on the inside of you? What comes naturally to you? Now is the time to discover your gifts. All you need for the journey ahead has already been given to you. Waste no more time observing others instead focus on you, then present what you have to God for multiplication to come forth.

Matthew 14 says that with just two loaves and five fish, Jesus fed over 5000 people. Jesus showcased the principle of multiplication here by showing that all we need to do is believe, present it before God and watch it multiply. God needs you and I to entrust Him with the little we have for multiplication to come. What is it you have with you?

Reflect on this and write down your strengths. Ask for grace and wisdom to apply it as originally intended by God, then act as led.

God bless you as you do so.

Devotional Ninety-Two

Trust the Process

¹¹Take no part in the worthless deeds of evil and darkness; instead, expose them. ¹²It is shameful even to talk about the things that ungodly people do in secret. ¹³But their evil intentions will be exposed when the light shines on them, ¹⁴for the light makes everything visible. This is why it is said, "Awake, O sleeper, rise up from the dead, and Christ will give you light." ¹⁵So be careful how you live. Don't live like fools, but like those who are wise. ¹⁶Make the most of every opportunity in these evil days.

(Ephesians 5:11-16 NLT)

Greetings to you my beloved family in Christ Jesus.

Where there is life, there is hope so hang in there for help is on the way. Cast all your cares upon the Lord and He will give you rest.

What does this mean? To cast your cares unto Him means that you intentionally entrust all that bothers you into God's hand knowing that He is mighty to save you from all your worries. You see, the problem is that we say we believe but when the test comes, we are too quick to break. Why do we worry when we have a supreme being on our side who knows and cares about every detail of our lives? Don't you know that worries lead to unnecessary sicknesses and pain? God is saying "Trust me"

Trust the process now that you are here on earth. Trust the process this year not next year. Now! You can't say you are mine and operate like one rooted in the kingdom of darkness. Now is the time to place all matters at His feet, one after the other. This is an act that we believers must practise on a day-to-day basis.

Believing that God is able can only occur when you truly know that you have a higher authority over you who is able to handle all matters. Now is the time to quit thinking God is far away from you. He is near and readily available to help those who truly call unto Him for help.

He said to me last night "Mbeloved, I am here for you". What about you? Ask Him for help and wait for His response. You must develop the act of waiting for God's response before moving. God speaks!

So, He has given you a vision, but you question how this would pan out. Don't you know that for every vision, there is provision if you truly master the art of waiting and trusting Him? God needs you and I to step into the place of maturity today. Come boldly before me and obtain favour saith the Lord of Heavenly Hosts. I am mighty to deliver you from every entanglement and enslavement. You must trust the process to see tangible results this season!

Devotional Ninety-Three

How You Enter Your Day Matters

¹³No, dear brothers and sisters, I have not achieved it, but I focus on this one thing: Forgetting the past and looking forward to what lies ahead, ¹⁴I press on to reach the end of the race and receive the heavenly prize for which God, through Christ Jesus, is calling us. ¹⁵Let all who are spiritually mature agree on these things. If you disagree on some point, I believe God will make it plain to you. ¹⁶But we must hold on to the progress we have already made.

(Philippians 3:13-16 NLT)

Greetings to you my beloved family in Christ Jesus.

Wake up today determined to make it count. Cast away all sorrow, fear and pain today and enter into the place of REST. Come and receive WINE from the throne room of mercy today. God is calling you to come up hither. COME!

Come forward forgetting the wrongs and pain of yesterday. Rise into victory knowing that you have a Father that can never fail. You have a Father that knows what is best and what you need. Rise up today knowing greater is He that is in you than He that is in the World. Quit believing the lies sold to you by the enemy. In fact, you have the power to eliminate every negative thought today by simply discarding it and rendering it useless. Now, begin to speak God's Word over your life. I am the child of the Highest God. I will not be silent for I know that my redeemer lives. Hallelujah!

Speak out today. Speak to yourself now! What can you do to make yourself smile today? I am determined to smile regardless of the happenings around me.

This is the day that the Lord has made. Quit talking about others instead focus on your canvas which represents your life and begin to paint. Yes, paint your world as best as you can. Discard the black and greys and use bright colours to paint your world. Let's have a look at God's canvas which is the world as we know it. Look at how bright the sky is. Gaze at the beauty of creation. That is our Father's work. Paint your world like He did and REST.

This is the time to create. Don't just sit there silent. Open your mouth and declare what you want to see. Don't give up until it becomes your reality. Encourage yourself in the Lord!

God bless you abundantly.

Devotional Ninety-Four

Pick Up Your Phone

¹²I know how to live on almost nothing or with everything. I have learned the secret of living in every situation, whether it is with a full stomach or empty, with plenty or little. ¹³For I can do everything through Christ, who gives me strength.

(Philippians 4:12-13 NLT)

Greetings to you my blessed family in Christ Jesus. Today is the day the Lord has made; we will rejoice and be glad in it. How has your day been? What you do with the remaining hours of the day is totally up to you. You either choose to use it wisely by handing it to the Holy Spirit to manage or allow it to pass you by doing all that seems right. The choice is yours!

The time has come to make out time to reach out to your family and friends. You cannot say you love but find it hard to call those you care about. On this path of righteousness, one must love intentionally and remain consistent. To love is a sacrifice and a selfless act.

As for me, I have determined in my heart to work on loving others by making out time to check up on their wellbeing. When you love, others will love you in return. Jesus spent His time on earth with the poor and needy. He paid close attention to the needs of the people and met every need. This is exactly how we ought to live our lives here on earth. To live a selfless life is paramount on this journey.

What do you spend your time doing?

Reflect on this question and allow the Holy Spirit to open your eyes to the truth.

Finally, monitor how you spend your time on a day-by-day basis by taking a log. Discipline and Wisdom are required for the management of one's time. Quit thinking about moving instead make a decision to move and do it.

God bless you.

Devotional Ninety-Five

The State of Your Heart

¹¹May you always be filled with the fruit of your salvation—the righteous character produced in your life by Jesus Christ—for this will bring much glory and praise to God. ¹⁹For I know that as you pray for me and the Spirit of Jesus Christ helps me, this will lead to my deliverance.

(Philippians 1:11, 19 NLT)

Greetings to you my beloved family in Christ Jesus. How are you holding up? Many are on the verge of breaking down. If this is you, I ask that you allow the Holy Spirit to help you stand this day. Breaking down is the easiest option instead why not determine in your heart to rise up against all odds. Rise unto higher grounds this day and be who God says you are.

Beating yourself up for the wrong of yesterday is a wasted effort. I encourage you this day to stand up with an intention to rejoice.

What is that matter you are currently dealing with this day? Run to the throne of grace and obtain mercy from God. As I went on my walk today, I noticed a fisherman sitting by the lake hoping to catch fish then I realised that Jesus targeted fishermen because of their zeal and perseverance. To be a fisherman means that one must be patient, tolerant, attentive, focused, persistent, determined etc.

Jesus's disciples were all of the above. They had what was required to finish the race. Jesus said to them come and I will teach you how to fish for men. You cannot come if you are not ready for change. God is ready to take you by the hand if you are willing to adhere to His instructions. Are you ready to wait on God? Are you ready?

Journey with the Holy Spirit today and allow Him to show you the way to go. Be intentional about all you do from today. Smile regardless! Rest from your worries and keep moving.

Finally, God is still in the business of turning lives around. Believe!

Devotional Ninety-Six

Take No Offense

¹³This will continue until we all come to such unity in our faith and knowledge of God's Son that we will be mature in the Lord, measuring up to the full and complete standard of Christ. ¹⁴Then we will no longer be immature like children. We won't be tossed and blown about by every wind of new teaching. We will not be influenced when people try to trick us with lies so clever they sound like the truth. ¹⁵Instead, we will speak the truth in love, growing in every way more and more like Christ, who is the head of his body, the church.

(Ephesians 4:13-15 NLT)

Greetings to you my beloved family in Christ Jesus. What is the state of your heart today? Now that is the million-dollar question. Do you know the true state of your heart? Check yourself!

It is our duty to examine our hearts on a day-by-day basis discarding every yeast. For a little yeast ferments the whole dough. Come closer and let us truly come clean. Are you who you say you are?

This is the question I asked myself today. Maria, are you truly one who loves God genuinely? Are you truly your brother's keeper? Do you go all out for your neighbours? Do you love as Christ loves? My answer is NO, I DON'T. I cannot truthfully say

I love as I should, but I know that I am a work in progress and one ready to learn as directed by the Holy Spirit.

What is the Holy Spirit saying today? Make excuses for the wrongs of all who offend you. Allow no yeast into your heart. Watch and pray at all times! Be alert with your lamp full of oil and extra. Remember that the enemy is going around looking for whom to devour, don't be another victim of the enemy. Rise out of your sleep and take charge!

You cannot say you are genuinely for the Lord and operate in anger. Regardless of what your enemy does, Scripture advises us to love back. You cannot give evil for evil. This is a lesson for all to note. You are not where you should be therefore, hold on to the Holy Spirit and allow Him to direct your path unto higher grounds. He will not act unless you ask for help. Do you need His help today? Ask!

When will you quit giving room to the devil in your heart? When will you stand and take charge? When will you stand for change? These are questions to meditate on. Go and sit with Jesus for clarity of purpose.

You are here to bring change!

Rise up for you might be the change the world needs today. Have a blessed day.

Devotional Ninety-Seven

Breathe

¹⁷On the other hand, don't be too wicked either. Don't be a fool! Why die before your time? ¹⁸Pay attention to these instructions, for anyone who fears God will avoid both extremes.

(Ecclesiastes 7:17-18 NLT)

Breathe away the sorrow and allow Christ to breathe new life into your mortal bodies. Yes, you have prayed and waited for that miracle, giving up is not an option. Keep waiting for your joy is around the corner.

Greetings to you my beloved family in Christ Jesus. Ever found yourself worried and confused? In fact, are you in a place of confusion today? Come to God this day ready for new oil and strength. Allow God to strengthen you afresh bringing you to a place of restoration and rejuvenation.

You have a reason to smile because God is still on your case. He is too good to fail you. Keep trusting and waiting on Him for that mighty testimony. Though it may tarry, it will surely come to pass at the appointed time.

Quit complaining and arguing over spilt milk. Yes, the past is nothing to write home about. Why not forget the past and look forward to that which the Lord has promised you? For He is still in the business of turning things around for your good. Just believe!

He said that the best is mine if I believe. What about you? Do you believe that He will change your story for good or are you relying on alternative solutions? I heard it clearly today whilst waiting that I mustn't sell myself short. Many would question whether it was God who spoke or myself, but I know my redeemer liveth.

My redeemer liveth. Yes, He lives, and He will turn things around for your good if you wait on Him trusting that He is able. View that dream plan again and see it manifest before your eyes. Now is the time to dream. Dream big for the Lord is able!

Have a blessed day.

Devotional Ninety-Eight

Change Your Circle

¹⁹May you experience the love of Christ, though it is too great to understand fully. Then you will be made complete with all the fullness of life and power that comes from God.

(Ephesians 3:19 NLT)

Who are the people you call friends? Birds of the same feather flock together. This saying is so true and many times all one needs to do is observe those you walk with and call friends.

Are you one going around with whoever you like without seeking God's face for clarity? Be careful lest you fall! This is a warning for those that have ears, quit running around with that friend who talks about crime casually or that one who sees no value in marriage or togetherness. Run or you will follow in their footsteps. Bible says, " Guard your heart with all diligence for out of it are the issues of life".

As a parent, you have a duty to observe and monitor your children's friends. Quit giving them the freedom to go about doing whatever they like instead lead and show them the way to go. Monitor their space in order to ensure they remain on the path of righteousness.

The time has come to take ownership of all around you. Quit giving excuses of what could have been, instead rise up and do the needful. Allow the Holy Spirit to lead you then act accordingly. The devil's job is to close your eyes to the truth, but Christ has come to give you a hope and future. Rise today and begin to see aright.

See the future and run in it. Walk away from toxic friends and carefully watch and pray in order to know what path to take. Do not become complacent or ignorant instead monitor your circle carefully so that you remain rooted in God's perfect will.

Now is the time when many pretend to be righteous to get into homes for the sole purpose of destruction. The righteous are awake and observant to the tricks and lies of the evil one. Habakkuk decided to climb to the watchtower in order to see and hear clearly from God. What about you?

The choice is yours. You either lay down with no care in the world or rise up to take charge of your world with the help of the Holy Spirit. Remember that the enemy is not sleeping, he goes around looking for whom to devour. Be very vigilant!

Devotional Ninety-Nine

Change Your View and Do the Needful

15As you know, you Philippians were the only ones who gave me financial help when I first brought you the Good News and then travelled on from Macedonia. No other church did this. 16Even when I was in Thessalonica you sent help more than once. 17I don't say this because I want a gift from you. Rather, I want you to receive a reward for your kindness. 19And this same God who takes care of me will supply all your needs from his glorious riches, which have been given to us in Christ Jesus.

(Philippians 4:15-17, 19 NLT)

I am determined to rise up today. What about you?

Greetings to you my beloved family in Christ Jesus. Isn't it easy to lay down there feeling sorry for oneself? Well, I am here to say it is the lazy option. Quit feeling sorry for yourself instead get busy. Get busy with the little you can do today and don't stop until you have achieved the task. Why are you downcast my friend? God has come to shed light on that dark patch today.

See the light at the end of the tunnel today and run towards it. For it is not over until God says it is over. Why have you lost hope in tomorrow? Don't you know that hope lost means you can never receive from the Lord, Why? Without hope, it's impossible to believe and have faith. You must first hope for a thing, believe it is possible then have faith that it will become your reality. God is calling you to rise up today.

Reach out to a friend or two today and encourage them to rise up. Observe your circle in order to know those who might be downcast or weary. Run away from the place of assumptions instead move as led today. Share a word or two with them and move to the next person. A sister shared this song with me a couple of days ago which lifted my Spirit: "Let there be love shared amongst us". I will not give up on you therefore don't give up on you.

The aim of this message is for every life to read it and hear God individually in order to receive their blessings from God. You must be blessed by what you read. Today's message is for you, yes you! Rise up and smile. Pick up yourself today and determine in your heart to make it count. Wipe the tears away my friend and allow the Holy Spirit in.

For the joy of the Lord is your strength. Unlimited joy is yours today in Jesus mighty name. Reflect not on the mistakes and flaws of yesterday. Quit dwelling on what isn't and start living today. Create a new path and walk in it joyfully.

Quit dwelling on what you don't have instead thank God for what you have and make it count.

Devotional One Hundred

Go Get It

⁹Young people, it's wonderful to be young! Enjoy every minute of it. Do everything you want to do; take it all in. But remember that you must give an account to God for everything you do. ¹⁰So refuse to worry, and keep your body healthy. But remember that youth, with a whole life before you, is meaningless.

(Ecclesiastes 11:9-10 NLT)

I was reminded by a close sister yesterday that all we can ever think, or desire is available if we believe. Why then do you limit yourself?

Greetings to you my blessed family in Christ Jesus. Why are you short-changing yourself? Why are you allowing the devil to rob you? Wake up from your sleep and grab all that is available.

You can truly have all you desire if you seek God first and believe it is possible. God is able to do exceedingly abundantly above all that we ask or think. I know many believers quote this scripture, but do we truly understand what God is saying? Do you?

Our Heavenly Father is God and King of the whole universe. Believers are from a kingdom where there is no lack but abundance. Now, if you are truly a citizen of that Kingdom, why then do you have a beggar mentality? Why are you short-changing yourself by thinking small? It is important to note that this is your only opportunity to showcase all that has been given unto you. Now is the time to dig deep in order to know and utilise all that God has given unto you.

I have decided to use all I have for my own benefit. It is up to you and I to broaden our dreams and desires as best as we can. If your dreams don't scare you then you haven't dreamt well. Now is the time to go back to that vision board and alter all. You are a true heir of the Kingdom of heaven therefore tap into the unlimited resources available unto you.

There's safety under the shadow of the Almighty. Rest in all that God has said and begin to cross boundaries you never believed you could cross. Take a leap of faith today and do the impossible. You have a God who never fails.

TRUST HIM ALL THE WAY. DREAM BIG! DREAM AGAIN!

Final Word

Every message in this devotional was divinely inspired by the Holy Spirit. My prayer is that it reaches every part of the globe "from North to South, East to West". I pray that lives will be transformed daily as they read the heart of the Father.

Luke 15:3–7 says…

"There once was a shepherd with a hundred lambs, but one of his lambs wandered away and was lost. So, the shepherd left the ninety-nine lambs out in the open field and searched in the wilderness for that one lost lamb. He did not stop until he finally found it. With exuberant joy, he raised it up, placed it on his shoulders, and carried it back with cheerful delight! Returning home, he called all his friends and neighbours together and said, 'Let's have a party! Come and celebrate with me the return of my lost lamb. It wandered away, but I found it and brought it home.'"

Jesus continued, *"In the same way, there will be a glorious celebration in heaven over the rescue of one lost sinner who repents, comes back home, and returns to the fold—more so than for all the righteous people who never strayed away."*

John 15:7-8 says…

If you remain in me and my words remain in you, ask whatever you wish, and it will be done for you. This is to my Father's glory, that you bear much fruit, showing yourselves to be my disciples.

Hosea 6:3-4 says...

Let us acknowledge the Lord; let us press on to acknowledge him. As surely as the sun rises, he will appear; he will come to us like the winter rains, like the spring rains that water the earth.

Now is the time to return to the Father and spend quality time with Him.

If you would love to know about this God "Jehovah", contact us on Twfgministry14@gmail.com

We are also trusting God for volunteers around the World to help spread the gospel of Jesus. If interested in joining this global team of believers, contact us via Email: Twfgministry14@gmail.com

Follow Maria on Instagram: Mbeloved_Twfg

www.mbeloved.org

Acknowledgement

Many thanks to the Almighty God for bringing this dream to fruition. I know and believe that this is only the beginning. For He said, "Open your mouth and I will fill it". Thank you Lord for the manifestation of your Word. I am truly grateful.

Special thanks to Pastor Debo Olatunde for encouraging me to write all that God was sharing with me on a daily basis. Without this push, nothing would have been done.

I would also like to thank my spiritual mentor, Pastor Sayo Akintola, who has faithfully nurtured and mentored me for over 15 years. I am so blessed to have you in my life sir. Thank you for your love and consistent prayers.

Finally, I would like to thank my Covenant Sister, Kemi Emmanuel and my family for their never-ending love and support. May God continue to bless you all.

God bless you all.

Printed in Great Britain
by Amazon